Graceful Beginnings

Short and Easy for Anyone New to the Bible

Pathways to a Joyful Walk

A Joy-Seeker's Guide to a Rewarding
Spiritual Life

MELANIE NEWTON

JOYFUL
WALK
BIBLE
STUDIES

We express our thanks to Michelle Burns, Ansie Twigge, Diana Bravenec, Diane Bohannan, Jennifer Brasnick, Lala Cano, Kim Newton, Laura Rauhauser, Marlyn Scott, Melodye Carlock, Pam Mayfield, Stacy Collins, and Tammie Johnston who served as editors for this study.

Pathways to a Joyful Walk: A Joy-Seeker's Guide to a Rewarding Spiritual Life

Published by Joyful Walk Press. Flower Mound, TX.

ISBN: 979-8-9925750-6-4

For questions about the use of this study guide or for bulk orders, please email us at melanienewton.com/contact.

Cover photo by John Newton, accessed at flickr.com (8162179887_0c6797557b_o.jpg), used by permission. Walkway graphic from clipartkey.com (448436.png) used by permission. "Joyful Walk" graphic adapted from flyclipart.com (15828994-1623267744398-561843ad6ba7a.jpg), used by permission.

Melanie Newton is the author of "Graceful Beginnings" books for anyone new to the Bible and "Joyful Walk Bible Studies" for established Christians. Her mission is to help women learn to study the Bible for themselves and to grow their Bible-teaching skills to lead others.

Joyful Walk Bible Studies are grace-based studies for women of all ages. Each study guide follows the inductive method of Bible study (observation, interpretation, application) in a warm and inviting format.

We pray that you will find *Pathways to a Joyful Walk* to be a resource that God will use to strengthen you in your faith walk with Him.

Grace-based • Christ-Focused • Bible-Rich

JOYFUL WALK PRESS
Flower Mound, TX

MELANIE NEWTON

Melanie Newton is a Louisiana girl who made the choice to follow Jesus while attending LSU. She and her husband Ron married and moved to Texas for him to attend Dallas Theological Seminary. They stayed in Texas where Ron led a wilderness camping ministry for troubled youth for many years. Ron now helps corporations with their challenging employees and is the author of the top-rated business book, *No Jerks on the Job*.

Melanie jumped into raising three Texas-born children and serving in ministry to women at her church. Through the years, the Lord has given her opportunity to do Bible teaching and to write grace-based Bible studies for women that are now available from her website (melanienewton.com) and on Bible.org. *Graceful Beginnings* books are for anyone new to the Bible. *Joyful Walk Bible Studies* are for maturing Christians.

Melanie Newton loves to help women learn how to study the Bible for themselves. She also teaches online courses for women to grow their Bible-teaching skills to help others—all with the goal of getting to know Jesus more along the way. Her heart's desire is to encourage you to have a joyful relationship with Jesus Christ so you are willing to share that experience with others around you.

Jesus took hold of me in 1972, and I have been on this great adventure ever since. My life is a gift of God, full of blessings in the midst of difficult challenges. The more I have learned and experienced God's absolutely amazing grace, the more I have discovered my faith walk to be a joyful one. I am still seeking that joyful walk every day...

Melanie

OTHER BIBLE STUDIES BY MELANIE NEWTON

Graceful Beginnings Series books for anyone new to the Bible:

A Fresh Start (basics for new Christians)
Painting the Portrait of Jesus (the Gospel of John)
The God You Can Know (the character of God)
Grace Overflowing (an overview of Paul's 13 letters)
The Walk from Fear to Faith (7 Old Testament women)
Satisfied by His Love (women who knew Jesus)
Seek the Treasure (study of Ephesians)
Pathways to a Joyful Walk (6 pathways to a life filled with joy)

Joyful Walk Bible Studies for growing Christians:

Adorn Yourself with Godliness (1 Timothy and Titus, also in Spanish)
Everyday Women, Ever Faithful God (Old Testament women, also in Spanish)
Connecting Faith to Life on Planet Earth (Genesis 1-11; Revelation)
Graceful Living (the essentials for a grace-based Christian life)
Graceful Living Today (a devotional journal for a joyful life)
Healthy Living (Colossians and Philemon)
Heartbreak to Hope (the Gospel of Mark)
Identity: Sticking to Your Faith in a Pull-Apart World (Ezra thru Malachi)
Knowing Jesus, Knowing Joy (Philippians, also in Spanish)
Live Out His Love (New Testament women)
Perspective (1and 2 Thessalonians)
Profiles of Perseverance (Old Testament men, also in Spanish)
Radical Acts (Acts)
Reboot, Renew, Rejoice (1 and 2 Chronicles)
The God-Dependent Woman (2 Corinthians)
To Be Found Faithful (2 Timothy)

Resources for leading others

Be a Christ-Focused Small Group Leader
Leap into Lifestyle Disciplemaking
Bible Study Leadership Made Easy (online video course)
Painting the Picture of Jesus (the "I Am's" of Jesus lessons)
Teaching Children the God They Can Know (the character of God)

Download our catalogue and get resources for your spiritual growth at melanienewton.com.

Contents

Introduction 1

Pathway #1 Start with Jesus 7

Pathway #2 Bask in the Grace of God 21

Pathway #3 Grasp Who You Are 33

Pathway #4 Choose Whom You Will Serve 47

Pathway #5 Claim Your Freedom in Christ 61

Pathway #6 Keep Moving Forward 75

The Believer's Identity in Christ 91

The Biblical Process for Dealing with Recognized Sin 95

The Holy Spirit's Empowering Presence 97

Sources 99

Introduction

GRACEFUL BEGINNINGS

The *Graceful Beginnings* books are Bible studies specifically designed for anyone new to the Bible—whether you are a new Christian or you just feel insecure about understanding the Bible. The short and easy lessons will introduce you to your God and His way of approaching life in simple terms that can be easily understood.

Just as a newborn baby needs to know the love and trustworthiness of her parents, the new Christian needs to know and experience the love and trustworthiness of her God. *A Fresh Start* is the first book in the series, laying a good foundation of truth for you to grasp and apply to your life. The other books in the series can be done in any order. At the end of the last lesson in this study, we give you a preview lesson for the next study in the series.

SOME BIBLE BASICS

Throughout these lessons, you will use a Bible to answer questions as you discover treasure about your life with Christ. The Bible is one book containing a collection of 66 books combined together for our benefit. It is divided into two main parts: Old Testament and New Testament.

The Old Testament tells the story of the beginning of the world and God's promises to mankind given through the nation of Israel. It tells how the people of Israel obeyed and disobeyed God over many, many years. All the stories and messages in the Old Testament lead up to Jesus Christ's coming to the earth.

The New Testament tells the story of Jesus Christ, the early Christians, and God's promises to all those who believe in Jesus. You can think of the Old Testament as "before Christ" and the New Testament as "after Christ."

Each book of the Bible is divided into chapters and verses within those chapters to make it easier to study. Bible references include the book name, chapter number and verse number(s). For example, Ephesians 2:8 refers to the New Testament book of Ephesians, the 2nd chapter, and verse 8 within that 2nd chapter. Printed Bibles have a "Table of Contents" in the front to help you locate books by page number. Bible apps also have a contents list by book and chapter.

The Bible verses highlighted at the beginning of each lesson in this study are from the New International Version® (NIV®) unless otherwise indicated. You can use any version of the Bible to answer the questions, but using an easy-to-read translation (CSB, NLT, NET, ESV) will help you gain confidence in understanding what you are reading. You can find all these translations in "The Bible App (from Life.Church)," in "Blue Letter Bible App," or on biblegateway.com.

This study capitalizes certain pronouns referring to God, Jesus and the Holy Spirit—He, Him, His, Himself—just to make the reading of the study information less confusing. Some Bible translations likewise capitalize those pronouns referring to God; others do not. It is simply a matter of preference, not a requirement.

NEW TESTAMENT SUMMARY

The New Testament opens with the births of John the Baptist and Jesus. About 30 years later, John challenged the Jews to indicate their repentance (turning from sin and toward God) by submitting to water baptism—a familiar Old Testament practice used for repentance as well as when a non-Jew (often called Gentiles) converted to Judaism (to be washed clean of idolatry).

Jesus, who is also known by the title "Christ," is God's Son, fully God and fully man. Jesus publicly showed the world what God is like and taught His perfect ways for 3 – 3½ years. After preparing 12 disciples to continue Christ's earthly work, He died voluntarily on a cross for mankind's sin, rose from the dead, and returned to Heaven. The account of His earthly life is recorded in 4 books known as the Gospels (the biblical books of Matthew, Mark, Luke and John named after the compiler of each account).

After Jesus' return to Heaven, the followers of Christ were then empowered by the Holy Spirit and spread God's salvation message among the Jews, a number of whom believed in Christ. The apostle Paul and others carried the good news to the Gentiles during 3 missionary journeys (much of this recorded in the book of Acts). Paul wrote 13 New Testament letters to churches & individuals (Romans through Philemon). The section in our Bible from Hebrews to Jude contains 8 additional letters penned by five men, including two apostles (Peter and John) and two of Jesus' half-brothers (James and Jude, whose mother was Mary). The author of Hebrews is unknown. The apostle John also recorded Revelation, which summarizes God's final program for the world. The Bible ends as it began—with a new, sinless creation.

ELEMENTS OF EACH LESSON

This book is a short and easy study covering the choices you need to make with your mind and your heart as a believer in Christ so that your lifelong faith walk will be a joyful one.

1. Each lesson begins with a Bible verse that relates to the focus of the lesson and a prayer. Prayer is just talking to God as conversation with someone who loves you dearly. The beginning prayer simply asks Jesus to teach you through the lesson.

2. This is followed by a description of the "PATHWAY" and simple study of the passages being covered by the lesson. Read the Bible verses and answer the associated questions. This study uses the NIV translation. We recommend you use that or other easy-to-read translations (CSB, NLT, NET, ESV). See "Bible Basics" above for online sources of these.

3. In the "THE PATHWAY TO JOY" section at the end of the study questions, you will be encouraged to dwell more on what you learned in the lesson that applies to your life today.

4. A short teaching session ("JOYFUL WALK") follows each lesson giving additional insight into the verses covered by the lesson plus application. You can listen to each of these as a podcast from melanienewton.com/podcasts. Look for "15: Joyful Walk" to find the one for each lesson. You can also find these podcasts on most podcast providers. Or you can read the blogs associated with the podcasts at melanienewton.com/blog. Choose Joyful Walk category then scroll to find the title you want. Listen to the first podcast as an introduction to the study.

5. Every "JOYFUL WALK" section is followed by a "REFLECT" time for you to respond to what you learned and some prayer prompts related to the lesson.

SMALL GROUP DISCUSSION

While you can work through these lessons as a personal study, this topic is perfect to use for small groups. Share the following suggested guidelines with the group members to maximize your discussion group experience.

➤ Set aside some time each week to do the study questions so that you will get to know God better.

- ➤ Consistently attend whether your lesson is done or not. You will learn from the discussion.

- ➤ Respect each other's insights. Listen thoughtfully. Share your own insights, but do not dominate the discussion.

- ➤ Celebrate unity in Christ by avoiding controversial subjects such as politics, divisive issues, and denominational differences.

- ➤ Maintain confidentiality of whatever is shared within the group.

Enjoy your small group discussion and learn from one another. As you journal parts of your story and share that with your group members, you will have a greater connection with each other. And you will have more reason to praise our ever-faithful God as you see and hear how He has been faithful to each of you through the years. A small group is a great place to share how you are seeking the treasure of Christ in your life. Discussing the lesson and the teaching session should take about an hour, making this an easy study to fit into a busy workday schedule.

Suggested Leader Guide for Group Discussion:

You can download a more detailed discussion guide at melanienewton.com/pathways-to-a-joyful-walk-bible-study. Or follow the suggestions below:

1. Pray for the Holy Spirit to teach you what He wants you to know through the lesson.

2. Work through the LESSON together, reading the Bible verses and discussing the questions. Predetermine which of the explanatory paragraphs you will read as a group.

3. Read the "THE PATHWAY TO JOY" summary and share responses to any included application questions.

5. Discuss parts of the "JOYFUL WALK" section that you want to emphasize. Or listen to the podcast together. "REFLECT" on the teaching.

6. Pray for the group members: Ask Jesus to satisfy your hearts through knowing Him. Thank God for His grace toward you and His love for you.

7. Remind each person to do the next lesson and listen to the related podcast before the group meets again.

PATHWAYS TO A JOYFUL WALK

What is the most enjoyable walk you have ever taken? Why was it so enjoyable? Was it the place where you were walking? Was it the person who was walking with you?

Did you know that the Bible calls your whole life a "walk" of faith? If you have trusted in Jesus Christ, you are now on a faith **walk**. Physical walking is a process of movement in a specific direction trusting your legs to support your body weight. Similarly, a faith walk is a process of moving forward with Jesus Christ by your side, learning to trust His strength to support you, and being rewarded with His joy. You must choose the right pathways to get there.

What are the right pathways?

A pathway is a way of achieving a specified result. Are you a joy-seeker? Then, you want a guide to the right pathways to find joy in your spiritual life. Biblical joy refers to a **deep inner gladness, regardless of the circumstances** going on around you. That means whether you are rich or poor, sick or healthy, successful or struggling, you can still have a feeling of gladness or pleasure deep down inside. Do you want that? That joy is yours as you choose the right pathways to take for your faith walk.

The pathways to joy are these:

1. Start with knowing Jesus Christ
2. Bask in God's marvelous grace to you
3. Grasp who you are as a Christian
4. Choose whom you will serve every day
5. Claim your freedom from bondage
6. Move forward with perseverance through every trial

The reward is a joyful walk with Christ for a lifetime.

Are you a joy-seeker? Let *Pathways to a Joyful Walk* be your guide to that rewarding spiritual life.

It is going to be a great journey. And I am so glad to be walking beside you!

Melanie Newton

Start with Jesus

The Word became flesh and made his dwelling among us. We have seen his glory, the glory of the one and only Son, who came from the Father, full of grace and truth. (John 1:14)

Recommended: Listen to the podcast "THE PROMISE OF A JOYFUL WALK" before doing this lesson to get some background for the whole study. Use the following listener guide.

THE PROMISE OF A JOYFUL WALK

The Bible refers to human life as a "walk." Although some days you may feel like yours is a sprint, your whole life experience is considered a walk. Those who place their faith in Jesus Christ are on a "faith walk." God acted. We respond to His action by saying yes to faith in Jesus Christ and jumping into the new life God has for us. Instead of believing in our own ability to earn God's favor, we now trust in what Christ has done for us. That is your faith walk.

The process of walking*

Walking is a process of moving forward, putting one foot in front of the other. Spiritual life is also a process of trusting God with one thing after another. Your salvation by faith in Jesus Christ is an instantaneous event. But living out that wonderful salvation in the light of God's grace takes the rest of your life.

Walking requires gaining confidence and trust, just as when toddlers learn to walk. Every Christian must learn how to trust God and learn from His Word to trust God on your faith walk.

Walking requires communication between the head and the body. Our brains control how our bodies function, relaying messages to our legs that are received and acted upon. You as a believer must trust your Head, Jesus Christ, and let Him lead you, teach you, and enable you to live a life that pleases Him and brings joy to you.

Walking is repeated. Muscles need to be fed and exercised daily. Likewise, your faith needs to be fed with God's Word and exercised through trusting God with something every day.

Walking requires choices. Consider the purpose for your walk and make the right choices (pathways) to accomplish that purpose.

Pathway = a way of achieving a specified result; a course of action

Pathways to a Joyful Walk lessons will guide you to the pathways for achieving a faith walk that is full of joy. That is the reward.

The gift of joy

If you are wanting a joyful walk, you need to be able to recognize what it means to be joyful or full of joy. Joy is often confused with a feeling of happiness that comes from "good happenings" that are **external**. Everything is going your way so you are happy. But when things are not going well, happiness often disappears.

For believers in Jesus Christ, we have access to a different kind of joy that is **internal**. This joy comes from within God Himself as part of His character. God takes great delight in those who trust in Him and even rejoices with singing over them (Zephaniah 3:17). God gives us His joy and uses that to make us strong (Nehemiah 8:10). Jesus gives us this same joy (John 15:11) in such abundance that those who "believe in Him are filled with an inexpressible and glorious joy" (1 Peter 1:8).

Biblical joy refers to a **deep inner gladness, regardless of the circumstances** around you. That means whether you are rich or poor, sick or healthy, successful or struggling, you can still have a feeling of gladness or pleasure deep down inside.

> ➢ Biblical joy is supernatural. It is inseparable from the character of God and comes only from a relationship with Him.

> ➢ Biblical joy is a fruit of the Spirit of Jesus living inside you and every other Christian. Joy is available to you (Galatians 5:22).

> ➢ Biblical joy is a deep abiding peace and sense of contentment and strength. You may not feel like smiling on the outside, but you can still smile on the inside. Have you ever felt that way?

Now that you know the definition of joy and understand how all of life is a walk, what would be a joyful walk? When you are on a joyful walk, you are accessing this deep, inner gladness and peace so that you can rest and rejoice in God no matter what is going on around you. All of that is yours as you choose the right pathways to take for your faith walk. We will cover those pathways in this series of lessons.

Let Jesus satisfy your heart with joy so that your daily walk with Him will be a joyful one.

*The process of walking adapted from "It's a Walk" accessed at MinTools.com.

PATHWAY #1

Picture in your mind an enjoyable walk that you took or would like to take with someone you love.

Who is that someone? Why do you love that person? What makes walking with that person enjoyable?

The same is true for your faith walk. **Pathway #1 is this: "Start with Jesus."** That means knowing who Jesus is and putting your faith in Him to be your Savior. This is a required pathway to have a joyful walk because you can only experience real joy through knowing Jesus. This is a walk with someone who loves you.

CHRISTIANITY IS CHRIST

The New Testament opens with the births of John the Baptist and Jesus. About 30 years later, John challenged the Jews to indicate their repentance (turning from sin and toward God) by submitting to water baptism—a familiar Old Testament practice used when non-Jews became Jews.

Shortly after that, Jesus presented Himself to the public. The account of His earthly life is recorded in the four books known as the Gospels—the biblical books of Matthew, Mark, Luke, and John named after the compiler of each account. Each Gospel presents Jesus as "the Christ," a title that comes from the Greek word *christos,* a translation of the Hebrew term "Messiah" meaning the "anointed one." The Old Testament prophets promised that the Messiah, as the anointed one of God, would come and do many wonderful things for God's people including restoring God's rule on earth.

Christianity is Christ! It is not a lifestyle, rules of conduct, or a society whose members are joined together by the sprinkling or covering of water. Christians are followers of Jesus who is the Christ. If you have heard the good news of the gospel and believed that Jesus is the Christ, the Son of God who gave Himself for your sins, you have eternal life just by believing in Him as your Savior. But even more than salvation, Jesus calls all humans into a close relationship with Himself as brothers, sisters, and friends.

Jesus is also our Lord, the one who sits at the right hand of His Father God as head over everything else in heaven and on earth. As Lord, Jesus Christ is our *master*—the one to whom we should willingly give our obedience. He is our *model* of how to live as humans in a dependent relationship with God, and He is our *mentor* in walking with us in that dependent relationship.

Jesus' disciples were just like us except they physically beheld the risen Jesus. We must see Him through eyes of faith and allow the four books revealing His life (Matthew, Mark, Luke, and John) to reveal our Lord to us. This is so that we may know this God-man who changed our lives as we received the Good News. We need to frequently read about His life, watch movies based on it, and tell the stories about Him to know His life well because Christianity is Christ!

What questions do you have about Jesus or Christianity?

WHO IS JESUS?

From the beginning of the New Testament, Jesus Christ was declared to be both fully human (as a descendant of Abraham and the Jewish king David) AND fully God—more specifically the Son of God.

Jesus is fully human.

Read Luke 1:28-33.

> *Jesus began His human life in whose human body (verse 31)?*

> *Jesus descended from whose earthly lineage (verse 32)?*

Read Luke 2:1-7, 21, 51-52.

What human experience did Jesus have (verses 6-7)?

What did He as a Jewish boy experience (verse 21)?

What is told of His human childhood (verses 51-52)?

Jesus is fully human. He experienced the normal process of body development from child to adult man. He obeyed His parents and learned to live with at least four brothers and two sisters (Mark 6:3). In His human body, Jesus felt hunger and thirst, sadness and anger, distress and pain.

Because Jesus was fully human, He understands every single one of the things you experience: your heartaches, physical pains, feelings of rejection, strained relationships, abuse, grief, and impatience. He also understands your joys as well.

Jesus is fully God.

Read John 5:17-21.

What did Jesus claim about Himself in verses 17-18?

What did Jesus claim about Himself in verses 19-20?

What did Jesus claim about Himself in verse 21?

In this "sermon," Jesus appeals to the audience to view the work He is doing as evidence that He has been sent by His Father (God). His listeners recognized that He claimed equality with God. He claimed authority over eternal life (future resurrection of believers). All those are strong claims! Only God has authority over eternal destiny. Like a lawyer trying a case, Jesus presented undeniable evidence that He is the promised Messiah who is the Son of God.

Read John 6:38-40.

What claims did Jesus make about Himself?

Read John 8:42.

What claims did Jesus make about Himself?

Read John 14:6-14.

What did Jesus declare about Himself in...

- verse 6?

- verses 9-10?

What authority did Jesus claim for Himself in verses 13-14?

Read Mark 2:1-12.

What authority did Jesus claim for Himself (verses 5 and 10)?

Did you catch all that Jesus claimed and did that only God could or would do? Jesus claimed to have come down from heaven and to have been sent by God the Father. This is a claim of pre-existence, that is, Jesus claimed to have existed before His human birth. Jesus then said that He was sent by His Father (God) to do the Father's will on earth. He said that anyone can know and see God through looking at Him and His life. He claimed the authority to forgive sins. Jesus was not just a good teacher. He claimed and demonstrated that He was God in human flesh.

Jesus claimed these truths for Himself in the gospels. He called Himself the Son of Man. His coming into human history did not suddenly burst upon an unsuspecting world. It fulfilled a long line of prophecies that started with Genesis 3:15. The arrival of Jesus in human form was planned before the creation of the world as was the mission He was sent to accomplish—reconciling the world to God.

Jesus is God the Son.

While confirming that there is only one true God, believers have worshiped Jesus Christ and have spoken of Him in terms appropriate only of deity from the earliest days of Christianity. The Holy Spirit is also known as deity. You may be confused how Jesus could be God and the Spirit could be God and the Father could be God. Who is the one that is really God? The answer is all of them: three-in-one.

The Bible clearly teaches three Divine Persons, each rightly called God, yet all are the one and same God—God the Father, God the Son (Jesus), and God the Holy Spirit. The doctrine of the *Trinity* (or "Tri-unity," a man-made label) is a summary of the teachings of the Bible regarding the nature of God.

Read Luke 3:21-22 (in the presence of John the Baptist and others).

When Jesus was baptized by John, who came down from heaven in recognizable form?

Who spoke from heaven? What did He say about Jesus?

Read Matthew 28:19-20 (Jesus' own words).

New believers were to be baptized in the names of whom (verse 19)?

Though difficult to understand in our human minds, the Bible clearly teaches that our God is **one in essence** (one God) **yet three in person** (Father, Son, Holy Spirit). We must accept that truth.

The people living in the very religious culture of that time held strongly to the belief that there is only one God. When Jesus called people to a spiritual relationship with Himself as well as with God the Father, it is no wonder that many of the Jewish leaders were shocked at what Jesus said. But Jesus demonstrated that what He claimed was indeed the truth. He was God the Son in human flesh.

Here is a key truth: The invisible God can be seen and known through His Son, Jesus Christ, who is both God and man.

What others recognized about Jesus

Read John 1:1-2, 14. John was one of the twelve Apostles.

What did John declare to be true about Jesus in...

- verses 1-2?

- Verse 14?

Read 2 Peter 1:16-18. Peter was one of the twelve Apostles.

Peter declared what truths about Jesus?

Read 1 John 1:1-3, also written by John the Apostle.

John declared what truths about Jesus?

The New Testament writers are consistent in their declarations that Jesus was truly God and not just a great teacher. If these writers knew that Jesus was not God and yet claimed that He was, you could say that they were liars, promoting a myth in order to somehow profit from it. But they did not do that. They declared what they had seen, heard, touched, and known to be absolutely true.

From the beginning, the Church (all Christians) has maintained that Jesus Christ, crucified and risen from the dead, is Savior and Lord of heaven and earth. His resurrected body was seen by more than 500 people and on at least six occasions (1 Corinthians 15:5-8). There were plenty of eyewitnesses to these truths.

THE PATHWAY TO JOY

Jesus Christ presented Himself as the answer to every need of the human heart. All the New Testament writers taught that truth also. Multitudes of people throughout the centuries have witnessed that He does indeed do what He promised for those who trust and follow Him.

Read Matthew 16:13-17.

What question did Jesus ask (verse 15)?

Jesus asked His disciples a question that is still the world's most important question: "Who do you say Jesus is?" Many want to tell you that He was just a great religious teacher. As we have seen in this lesson, Jesus Christ claimed equality with God. Either He was God, or He was not God. If He was not God, then He was a liar (meaning He knew He was not God but claimed it anyway) or a lunatic (meaning He thought He was God). Either way, you must decide.

Who do you say that Jesus is?

Jesus Christ is who He claimed to be. **Knowing Jesus Christ is the first pathway to joy** and the single most important issue in all of life.

KNOWING JESUS CHRIST

Recommended: Listen to the podcast "KNOWING JESUS CHRIST." Use the section below as a listener guide.

Just like physical walking is a process of movement in a specific direction using our legs, a faith walk is also a process of moving toward trusting God enough to rely on Him more than on yourself. It is dependent on open communication between what you know about God in your head and what you believe about Him in your heart. Your faith walk is influenced by daily choices of where you will go. The pathways you choose determine whether your faith walk will be a joyful one or not.

When it comes to joy, our God offers us something more lasting than the world's idea of happiness. Biblical joy is a **deep inner gladness, regardless of the circumstances** going on around you. It is supernatural, bringing to you a deep abiding peace and sense of contentment and strength. This kind of joy only comes to you through knowing Jesus Christ.

Know Jesus as the God who can meet your needs.

You may have heard people say, "Jesus never claimed to be God." But you now know that is not true. When you look at the text of the first four books of the New Testament which tell of Jesus' life, you can see that Jesus openly claimed to be God. You looked at just a few of those claims in this lesson. Jesus consistently called God His Father. He declared His right to judge and said that He deserves the honor that belongs to God. Those are pretty radical statements. The works He was doing could only be done by God.

In His trials before the Jewish and Roman leaders, Jesus did not defend Himself against the accusations being made against Him. But He did speak clearly and boldly to claim His identity as the promised anointed one of God. He claimed to be the Son of Man who was also the Son of God (Mark 14:61-64).

All God's powers and attributes are in Jesus. Nothing is missing. You cannot get any more of God apart from Jesus (Colossians 1:19; 2:9). Jesus Christ is fully God and is Lord over all. In the New Testament, Jesus is called the Lord Jesus Christ. Christ is His title. It comes from the Greek word *christos,* which translates the Hebrew title "Messiah" meaning "anointed one." According to Psalm 110:1, the Messiah would sit at the right hand of God and be called Lord. Jesus claimed this for Himself and is now sitting at God's right hand. Jesus is the Christ and the Lord. He is powerful enough to meet your needs.

Know Jesus as a human who understands your needs.

Jesus is fully human. We have a harder time wrapping our brains around **that** fact than we do believing He was God. Yet, Jesus experienced the normal process of body development from baby to adult man. He obeyed His parents and learned to live with at least six siblings. In His human body, Jesus felt hunger and thirst. Tears fell down His cheeks when His friends were hurting. He had the normal human emotional response of anger against the stubborn hearts of the religious people who opposed Him and were not teachable. During the last hours before His death, He experienced distress and pain just as you and I would. He was completely human while being completely God. None of us can really understand how this is, but we must accept it as truth.

Because Jesus was fully human, He understands every single one of your heartaches. He experienced human life for more than thirty years. He understands your physical pain, feelings of rejection, and strained relationships. He understands your abuse, grief, and impatience because those were part of His life as well.

Jesus looked upon the crowds of people who surrounded Him with compassion. He knew they had heartaches and pain and were filled with uncertainty about their future. Jesus not only felt their need but also wanted to do something about it and acted as needed.

The Lord Jesus also demonstrated in His life on earth how much He loved and valued women. He taught them truth about God, forgave them for their sins, accepted them in His circle of followers, and gave new life to them after His resurrection. His care for them was so countercultural to what they had previously known. Women recognized that and responded with love for Him and a desire to serve Him. Jesus Christ entered into the midst of their lives, visibly representing God to them, loving them dearly, and changing their lives forever! He does the same for you and me today.

Jesus was fully human, but He did not sin. He was able to do that because He loved God perfectly. He lived in perfect dependence on God the Father and in perfect obedience to His Father. We cannot live a sinless life as He did. Yet, He experienced every temptation to sin that we experience. He understands all the challenges we face. And in His life, He gave us a pattern to follow so that we can learn to love God, to depend upon Him by faith, and to live in obedience to Him.

Because Jesus is the God-man, you can be confident of two things. (1) As fully human, He understands how you feel. (2) As fully God, He is powerful enough to take care of your every need. When you go to Him in prayer, you can trust that He understands, that He knows how you are feeling, and that He knows your needs at that moment. You can trust His compassion for you to meet your needs. Are you confident of that?

Your joyful walk begins with knowing Jesus.

> God wants you to follow His Son. But you won't follow someone you don't trust. You can't trust someone you don't know, and you cannot know Christ apart from His Word. (Rebecca Carrell, heartstrongfaith.com)

The more you trust Jesus, the more you experience His joy. Jesus wants His joy to be in you abundantly.

> *I have told you this so that my joy may be in you and that your joy may be complete (John 15:11)*

Peter was one of those listening to Jesus' words. He recognized that what Jesus promised, He also fulfilled.

> *Though you have not seen him, you love him; and even though you do not see him now, you believe in him and are filled with an inexpressible and glorious joy... (1 Peter 1:8)*

"Though you have not seen Him." That refers to us today. You and I have not seen Him physically on this earth. But the moment you believe in Jesus Christ, the Holy Spirit comes to live inside of you and fills you with God's glorious, uncontainable joy.

My joyful walk began when I put my faith in Jesus Christ as my Savior by trusting in what He said about Himself and believing that He died on the cross for me. Are you confident that you have made the choice to put your faith in Jesus? If not, you can do so right now. Please consider praying this prayer along with me:

> Thank you, God, for loving me and for sending Your Son Jesus to die for my sins. I trust in Jesus Christ to be my personal Savior. I accept your gift of forgiveness for my sins. I turn my life over to You. Thank you for your goodness to me and your gift of eternal life. Amen.

If you did that, tell someone. As soon as you trust in Christ to be your Savior, you begin a loving relationship with Him. You begin your faith walk. You receive complete love and acceptance by God as your Father. You receive treasure that is yours to know and experience for the rest of your earthly life. When you trust in Christ, He is in your life forever. You will never be without Him. Ever.

Let Jesus satisfy your heart with joy so that your daily walk with Him will be a joyful one.

Reflect

Read and reflect on the lyrics to this beautiful song about Jesus.

> You were the Word at the beginning, One with God the Lord Most High. Your hidden glory in creation Now revealed in You our Christ. What a beautiful Name it is, The Name of Jesus Christ my King. What a beautiful Name it is, Nothing compares to this. What a beautiful Name it is, The Name of Jesus.
>
> You didn't want heaven without us So Jesus, You brought heaven down. My sin was great, Your love was greater, What could separate us now? What a wonderful Name it is, The Name of Jesus Christ my King. What a wonderful Name it is, Nothing compares to this. What a wonderful Name it is, The Name of Jesus.
>
> Death could not hold You, The veil tore before You, You silenced the boast of sin and grave. The heavens are roaring, The praise of Your glory, For You are raised to life again. You have no rival, You have no equal. Now and forever, God You reign. Yours is the kingdom, Yours is the glory. Yours is the Name above all names.
>
> What a powerful Name it is, The Name of Jesus Christ my King
> What a powerful Name it is, Nothing can stand against
> What a powerful Name it is, The Name of Jesus.
>
> (*What a Beautiful Name*, Words and Music by Ben Fielding &
> Brooke Ligertwood)

Pray: *Thank God for sending His Son so you can know Him. Tell Jesus you want to know Him well and trust Him daily. Ask Him to help you do that and to help you recognize anything that draws you away from Him.*

Bask in the Grace of God

For it is by grace you have been saved, through faith—
and this is not from yourselves, it is the gift of God—not
by works, so that no one can boast. (Ephesians 2:8-9)

Pray: Lord Jesus, please teach me through this lesson.

PATHWAY #2

Picture in your mind a walk you took when you enjoyed the sunshine. Maybe you were cold, and the sun's warmth felt so good. Or perhaps you had been cooped up inside your house and finally got to be outside in the fresh air and sunshine.

What did you experience? How did you feel?

Whenever I have taken a walk like that, I basked in the bright sunshine and fresh air as I experienced freedom from my confinement. To bask means to savor it, luxuriate in it, and soak it up. That is what we can experience, too, as we bask in God's grace for us and live luxuriously in the freedom He provides for us. **Pathway #2 is "Bask in the Grace of God."**

UNDERSTANDING THE GOSPEL MESSAGE

The ultimate grace gift, Jesus Christ, came. But why did He come? What was His purpose?

Since the days of Genesis 3, the one question that continually demands an answer is, "How can a guilty, sinful human be made right in the eyes of a holy God?"

The spiritual problem of every person can be compared to death caused by a fatal disease. Sin is "the disease" (Romans 3:23). Death is the "result of the disease" (Romans 6:23). Our two-fold problem demanded a two-fold solution. The Gospel message included the answer to both spiritual problems.

(1) For the problem of sin, people need forgiveness and righteousness. *God's answer: Jesus'* **death** *on the cross.* We can now be cured of the disease.

(2) For the problem of death, people need regeneration (the restoration of life). *God's answer: Jesus'* **resurrection** *from the dead.* We can now be given life that is forever.

The following quote captures the gospel message in a nutshell:

Jesus Christ **laid down** His life **for** you...so that He could **give** His life **to** you...so that He could **live** His life **through** you. (Major Ian Thomas, *The Saving Life of Christ*)

The sin disease

Our God is a holy God. That means He is completely separated from anything that is sinful or evil. There is no sin in Him at all. He is perfect. It is a unique part of His character—who He is. Humans are not without sin.

Read Jeremiah 17:9.

How is the human heart described?

Read Romans 3:23.

What is true about every human?

Read Romans 1:18-25.

How is this human sin sickness described (verses 18 and 25)?

What is being revealed from heaven against such sickness (verse 18)?

The desperately wicked and deceitful heart describes the sickness that is part of every human. Thus, there is an infinite gap between God's holiness and humanity's sinfulness. The Bible says that people willingly suppress the truth (you have probably seen this in your own life) and exchange the truth about God for a lie. Such sickness leads to destructive behavior. It also leads to physical death and separation from a holy God because of sin. Not a pretty picture, but that is a reality we must all face.

God's wrath against sin

Because God is holy, He takes action against sin. The Bible calls that "God's wrath." God's wrath is not a mood or a fit of temper like our experience with human anger. God's disposition toward sin and evil in His creation is as constant and unrelenting as His love and goodness. He hates and rejects evil with a perfect and holy anger. He will never bend or compromise. His own nature demands that He judge evil through action. **To preserve His creation God must destroy whatever would destroy it.** This is His righteous, holy wrath (Romans 1:18).

Let us put this in everyday terms. How much do you hate germs like the flu virus infiltrating your home? My disposition toward the flu virus is wrath. It is pollution of my home. I use a disinfectant to clean with gusto to keep my family from getting sick. Or consider an ant infestation in your home. Do you invite them in and ignore their presence while they take over your kitchen or bedroom? You likely do whatever you can to attack their presence and restore your home. That is expressing wrath against their destruction of your safe home environment.

God's wrath is more serious, of course. Sin has far more destructive consequences than the flu virus or ants. But you get the idea. God's love for His creation requires punishment for sin in order to destroy it. The punishment for sin is death (Genesis 3:19).

When Jesus was on earth teaching the Jewish people, He continually had to remind them about their greatest enemy—their sin. The Jews thought that their enemy was Rome and longed to be out from under the occupation. But their true enemy was their sin. The sacrificial system was not sufficient to get rid of human sin and change their hearts to be in tune with God and His purpose for their lives. They needed a Savior from their sin.

The same is true for us today. Our culture tends to dismiss the seriousness of human sinfulness. We blame people and circumstances for our behavior and attitudes rather than our deceitful, sin-sick hearts. We think that if we could only fix this or that, we would be happy and less stressed, and could pursue lives of purpose. Yet, our sinfulness will accompany us into the next situation or relationship.

Are you more likely to blame someone or something for your unhappiness or stress than your own sinfulness? Why?

Do you now understand God's wrath against all sinfulness? Do you understand that sin is not just things you see others do that you do not like? Ask Him to help you see human sin through His eyes.

THE CROSS: GOD'S SOLUTION TO THE SIN ISSUE

People in Old Testament times received acceptance from God and eternal life in the same way as we do today—by **faith** in the merciful grace of God. To deal with their sin disease, God in His mercy prescribed animals to die as substitutes to pay the penalty for human sin. The death of the animal was a sad and ugly thing just as sin is a sad and ugly thing. But the innocent animal's sacrifice provided forgiveness for human sin and opened the way for a person to have a restored relationship with a holy God. Even that was a temporary solution to the problem of sin and had limitations. Our merciful God had a solution planned that would be so much better than those animal sacrifices—giving His own Son.

Read Mark 8:31.

What did Jesus teach about God's plan for Him?

Read Mark 10:45.

Jesus said He came to do what?

Read 1 Peter 2:24.

What did Jesus do and why?

Read Romans 5:8.

How did God demonstrate His love for us?

Jesus understood His purpose—to give His life for all humanity. This was no surprise to Him or to God the Father who sent Him. It was God's plan all along. Jesus knew He would accomplish His purpose through His death and resurrection. Jesus bore our sins in His own body. By His wounds, we are healed of our sin disease. He did this so that we might die to sin and live for righteousness. What a change in life strategy for us! Isn't God's act of love for ungodly humans while we were still enemies such an amazing thing?!

For the problem of sin, people need sin to be removed and replaced with righteousness. *God's answer: Jesus' death on the cross.* Because of His finished work on the cross, we can now be cured of the sin disease. Sin no longer has the same power over us as it once had.

But like any disease that is cured, how good is that if you are dead? We have a fatal sin disease. "Fatal" means you are dead. That refers to spiritual death on earth and separation from God for eternity. For the problem of death, people need the restoration of life. *God's answer: Jesus' resurrection.*

THE RESURRECTION: GOD'S SOLUTION TO THE LIFE & DEATH ISSUE

Repeatedly, Jesus taught that He would not only be killed, but He would also rise again in three days. He did that. His resurrection is recorded in the books about Jesus' life (Matthew 28; Mark 16; Luke 24; and John 20) and verified in historical references.

Read 1 Corinthians 15:3-8.

What truth was repeatedly shared about Jesus (verses 3-4)?

Who were the eyewitnesses to this truth (verses 5-8)?

Paul confirms what was being taught everywhere about Jesus: that He died for our sins, that He was buried, and that He was raised from the dead—all according to what was promised in the Scriptures. His resurrected body was seen by more than 500 people at one time and on at least six occasions—plenty of eyewitnesses to these truths.

Do you believe that Jesus was resurrected from the dead as the Scriptures and all the eyewitnesses attest? As we will see in the next verses, that is an essential element of your faith walk as a Christian.

Read Romans 8:11.

Because of Jesus' resurrection, who is living in you?

Read 1 Peter 1:3.

Because of Jesus' resurrection, what do you receive?

Read 2 Corinthians 5:17.

Through your faith in Christ, what is now true of you?

For the problem of death, people need the restoration of life. *God's answer: Christ's resurrection.* We can now be given life that is forever. That life comes by way of the Holy Spirit who indwells every Christian. Jesus' resurrection provided the way for us to get that new life which will never be taken away because of our sin.

God gives life to everyone who believes. Salvation is described as being born again and receiving "life." We use the English word "regeneration" to describe this. Regeneration means simply a new birth, a new beginning, or a new order. Everyone who believes in Christ is made into a new creation the moment they believe.

What God set out to do for humans, He accomplished.

THE PATHWAY TO JOY

For any person, all that is required to benefit from what Jesus accomplished is to believe or trust in Him.

Read 1 John 5:11-13.

What can you know for sure (verse 13)?

Why (verses 11-12)?

Did you know that you could have this assurance of your salvation?

Knowing this assurance, how does it make you feel?

You can know for sure that God has given you eternal life through faith (belief) in His Son. Assurance of salvation can be known and experienced by (1) clearly understanding the gospel and (2) trusting God's promises in Jesus Christ. Assurance is not confidence in your own ability to hold on to Christ but confidence in *Him* and His promises to hold on to you!

Basking in God's grace is the second pathway to joy.

BASKING IN GOD'S GRACE

Recommended: Listen to the podcast "BASKING IN GOD'S GRACE." Use the section below as a listener guide.

God acted to rescue us from our wretched condition.

The Bible says that every human is born into the kingdom of darkness. And we have a spiritual enemy who keeps people in that **darkness** by **blinding** their minds so that they cannot see the light of the gospel (2 Corinthians 4:4). Those living in this darkness are chained to the ways of the world, to the spiritual powers of evil, and to their own sinful natures. It is a wretched condition.

But God's love for people and His mercy toward us led Him to take action to end our wretched condition. Because of that love, He sent His Son to earth to live as a human without sin and to offer Himself as a sacrifice for sin once and for all. Never again would an animal need to die for human sin. Jesus Christ did that for us on the cross.

Crucifixion was ugly. It was a place of agony and disgrace. The beautiful Son of God voluntarily experienced the ugliness of sin and took on its punishment for our sakes.

Crucifixion provided the best scenario for Jews and non-Jews alike because both groups participated in the sinful act of executing God's Son (Acts 2:23). It was God's plan for His Son to die on that cross for all of humanity's sin. No human being would ever come up with that plan. It requires faith alone.

It was God's plan to raise His Son from the grave with a new body. Jesus' resurrection provided the way for us to get new life that would never be taken away again because of our sin. The Jews believed in a future resurrection. The non-Jews thought it was nonsense. To them, no one would ever want to have another body once you got rid of yours.

The belief in Jesus' bodily resurrection from the dead requires faith alone, which is exactly what God wanted.

By God's GRACE, you are SAVED through your FAITH.

Three words associated with God's plan are more powerful than any of the forces holding anyone in darkness, skepticism, and unbelief. Those three powerful words are grace, saved, and faith. They explain the basis of your salvation and why you can be confident in it.

> *For it is by **grace** you have been **saved**, through **faith**—and this is not from yourselves, it is the gift of God—not by works, so that no one can boast. (Ephesians 2:8-9)*

God gives His GRACE.

Grace is undeserved favor. It is God giving favor to someone not because they are good enough to deserve it but because His love chooses to do so. God's grace springs from God's love. Grace provides this relationship with God. You cannot earn it by doing good works. Rather, it is a free gift from God that you accepted when you received Christ through faith.

Our faith begins with receiving the love of God and understanding it in the Gospel. "We love because he first loved us (1 John 4:19)." Many Christians do not know about God's love. That is why theology is important because a goofed-up theology is going to keep you from ever loving God. If you think you have to earn your way to heaven, you might be trying really hard. But you are never going to really love God. When we start with how much God loves us, we then see His love in His grace to us and forgiveness of all our sins. By God's grace to us, we are saved.

By God's grace, you are SAVED.

To be saved means "to be rescued or spared from disaster." God saves us from the darkness of sin and also from His own judgment against sin (physical death and spiritual separation from Him). That is what salvation means. We are rescued by our faith in Jesus Christ. And we are made alive so we are no longer spiritually dead. That happens the moment you place your faith in Jesus Christ.

You are saved through FAITH in Jesus Christ.

What is faith? Faith is not a blind belief or mindless gullibility. It is not being passive and doing nothing. Faith is also not a religious feeling like a tingle or a good feeling from performing some ritual.

So if faith is not that, what is it? The word "faith" means a "belief, trust, and commitment of mind and heart to something or someone."

- ➢ Faith is **intelligent**. That means first you need to know about that something or someone. It is based on information about the object of your faith.

- ➢ Faith is also **decisive**. It involves assent or agreement that the information about that someone or something is true.

- ➢ Faith **requires an act of the will**. Any conscious choice that involves trust, reliance, or dependence on someone or something requires a deliberate action to choose to trust the information.

Simply put, faith is placing your trust in God and His Word. It is a full commitment to Christ. When you received Christ, you put your trust in Christ and His death for your sin. You also trust that He was resurrected from the dead to give you His life. Instead of believing in your own ability to earn God's favor, you now trust that you have been reconciled to God through what Christ has done for you.

By God's grace, you are saved through your faith. It is by your faith in Christ alone that you are rescued from your blindness, darkness, and deadness.

God rescues you from the destruction caused by sin. He offers you this salvation by His grace that is given to you. It is the gift of God—not by works, so that no one can boast of their efforts. Your response to God's gift of rescue is to say, "Yes. I accept." That is a response of faith. You can know that you are saved by God's grace through your faith in His Son Jesus Christ." No doubts about it!

God makes ugly beautiful.

We cannot think ourselves out of the ugliness of our sin. Every bit of our sin is so ugly to God. It is as ugly as the most heinous crime that comes to your mind and as ugly as the crucifixion. But our redemption is absolutely beautiful. God is in the business of making ugly beautiful. He does that in many ways.

Because of Jesus' death on the cross, believers are cleansed of all sin and made new creations of life when God plants His Spirit within us. We are made alive as Christ is alive. That is beautiful.

Because of Jesus' resurrection from the dead, God gives you eternal spiritual life from the moment you believed. And you have complete acceptance before a holy God by faith alone. That which stood against you, the ugliness of your sin, is gone. Christ's life is given to you. He is living in you. That is beautiful.

When we die, we now have hope of eternal life in the presence of God so physical death is no longer to be feared. Jesus frees us from the fear of death.

No one doing this study is from a rougher background than those who lived in New Testament times. Did you grow up being deceived? Were you mistreated? Do you still struggle with relying on your own power to make your way in the world? Jesus Christ came to rescue you from that condition.

But God's grace is not just for salvation. It is for everyday living. The Bible describes God's grace as being abundantly poured out on those who desperately need Him and respond to Him by faith. That is an ongoing action on God's part. Hooray for that. I am one who desperately needs Him. So are you.

To bask means to savor it, luxuriate in it, and soak it up. It is like the warm and bright sunshine you experienced during the walk described at the beginning of this lesson. Or imagine standing beneath a cool waterfall on a hot, summer day. God's grace is like that unending flow. And with that grace come so many blessings and benefits.

You can **bask in God's grace** for you and the beauty of Christ's life in you.

Let Jesus satisfy your heart with joy so that your daily walk with Him will be a joyful one.

Reflect

What ugliness in your life has God made beautiful because of Jesus Christ living in you? Are you basking in His grace toward you? Let your heart sing out gratefully to Him.

Pray: Thank God for the gospel and His plan to heal you of your sin disease and to give you His life. Thank Him for what He has done to change the ugliness in your life to something beautiful. Ask Him to help you see His grace being poured out on you abundantly in your everyday life.

Grasp Who You Are

Therefore, if anyone is in Christ, the new creation has come: The old has gone, the new is here! (2 Corinthians 5:17 NAS)

Pray: Lord Jesus, please teach me through this lesson.

PATHWAY #3

Picture in your mind one of your favorite places to walk—a place that is very familiar to you. You know all the spots where you have to watch your step. Maybe there is a bench to sit and rest a bit or a special place to see a sunrise or a sunset.

What details would you use to describe this walk to someone who has never been on it?

All those details gave that walk an **identity**.

In our world, identity drives everything about life. You likely carry some kind of identity card (ID) with you—a driver's license or a work-related card. What is on it? Usually, it is your name and picture, some identifying characteristics like address or job title, and the authority that issued the ID to you. Your signature may be on the card representing your choice to enter into contract with the issuing authority. If someone asked, "Who are you?" you could answer with the information on that card.

Identities tell us who we are, where we live, how and where we can travel. Our identity drives what we can buy with our finances and qualifies us for employment. That is why it is devastating to have it stolen!

Knowing your spiritual identity is even more important. How you see yourself as a person directs how you live out your faith walk. You must grasp and hold onto your spiritual identity as tightly as you would your passport when you travel to a foreign country. **Pathway #3 is this:**

"Grasp Who You Are." You need to know who you are as a Christian and hold fast to it.

A NEW IDENTITY THAT ROCKS THE WORLD

When you trusted in Christ, you received a new spiritual identity. But do not expect the culture to validate your new identity. From a worldly point of view, you and I are the same as we have always been. All our "baggage" is still seen hanging around our necks. But the FACT is that every Christian is a new creation with a new identity in Christ. This new identity declares how God, who is our authority, now views us! It is what He has done for us and to us that really counts, not what the culture thinks of us or what we think of ourselves. And there are wonderful perks that go along with this new position in life.

You have learned how your faith in Jesus Christ sets you free from your previous sin-stained existence to enjoy a new life. But your ability to live out this freedom depends upon your understanding of who you now are and holding onto that truth.

The basis of identity

Think of some ways you try (or have tried in the past) to establish your identity apart from Christ.

> *What happens when you try to determine who you are by those things?*

From God's point of view, there are two kinds of people in the world: (1) those who are **in Adam** and (2) those who are **in Christ**.

Read 1 Corinthians 15:21-22.

> *What are the differences between being in Adam and being in Christ (verse 22)?*

Read Romans 5:12, 15-19.

What came to all people descended from Adam...?

- Verse 12—

- Verse 16—

What do those who are now in Christ (believers) receive?

- Verse 17—

- Verse 18—

- Verse 19—

Who you are "in" determines your identity and your inheritance.

(1) To be **in Adam** means that you have inherited his nature (sinful), the consequences of his actions (condemnation), and his destiny (death).

(2) To be **in Christ** means that you have inherited His nature (righteous), the consequences of His actions (justification), and His destiny (eternal life).

God has given you a new identity.

Read 2 Corinthians 5:17.

Being in Christ, what is true of you now?

Read Romans 6:1-6.

The word translated *baptized* (verse 3) came from the process for dyeing cloth. It did not matter if the cloth was sprayed, dipped, or immersed. The significance was taking on the **identity** of the dye. The reference to baptism in this passage refers to Spirit Baptism. Although water baptism is a picture of what the Spirit does to us, there is no mention of water in this passage. Spirit Baptism is much more significant and has far greater effects. In Spirit Baptism, we are "dyed" with Christ. The practical outcome is a total identification (uniting) with Him.

You were baptized (identified with Christ) in what experiences and why (verses 3 and 4)?

You are also what with Him (verse 5)?

The Greek word translated "united" literally means, "to make to grow together, to fuse." Being united with Christ, therefore, means that you become *fused together with Him.* That cannot be undone.

BENEFITS OF BEING IDENTIFIED WITH CHRIST

The moment you believed, the old self that was born **in Adam** died. A new self with the same body but a new interior started life as a new person with a new nature and a new inheritance. This means you can never go back to being in Adam. You will always be **in Christ.** Always!

Your new identity in Christ contains roughly thirty-six characteristics or benefits (see pages 111-114). You receive **all of these benefits at once** at the moment of your salvation because you are **in Christ**. God is not a vending machine, parceling out these benefits one at a time based on your performance. They are God's gifts to you based on His love for you. What God does to you is His choice, not yours. These benefits are **unconditional**. The burden of performance is upon God, not upon you.

In this lesson, we will cover just a few aspects of your new identity in Christ. These are true about you because of Christ's finished work on the cross and His resurrection.

Read Romans 5:9-10.

You are now what (verse 9)?

You are also now what (verse 10)?

In those two verses are 3 aspects of your new identity. You are **justified**. That means you are declared righteous and no longer guilty of your sin. You are **saved from the wrath of God**. That means that His anger against sin was satisfied by Jesus' death on the cross. He is no longer angry at your sin or at you. You are **reconciled**. That means your relationship with God is restored and is no longer broken. You have direct and instantaneous access to Him.

Read Titus 2:11-14.

What did Christ do to us and why (verse 14)?

Read Colossians 1:13-14.

What is true of you now?

Read Colossians 1:21-22.

What is true of you now (verse 22)?

Read 1 Corinthians 6:11.

What is true of you now?

In those verses are 3 more aspects of your new identity. You are **redeemed**. That means you are released from wickedness and no longer in bondage to sin. You are completely **forgiven** and no longer burdened by your sin and guilt. You are **sanctified**. That means you are perfected in God's eyes (holy, without blemish and free from accusation) and no longer flawed because of your sin. God continues to work in your life with the goal that your behavior will eventually look more like that of His Son. This will be evident as you yield to His transforming power in you.

From what we have already covered in Lesson 2 and this lesson, you can add that you are **born again**, **given new life**, and made into a **new creation** (1 Peter 1:3, Romans 8:9, and 2 Corinthians 5:17). There is one more you need to know for your joyful walk.

Read Ephesians 5:1.

What are you called?

You are a **dearly loved child of Go**d. Beloved. The word used there is the same word God uses for His Son in Mark 9:7. You are that loved!

THE PATHWAY TO JOY

One of the fundamental questions of the human race is that of identity, "Who am I?"

From a worldly point of view, you are viewed the same as you have always been—with the baggage still hanging around your neck. But you can know your true identity—what God has done to change you from the inside out. And knowing your true identity sets you free from the world's constraints and expectations. You are set free from your past. You are set free from the garbage that others feed you about your failures!

Here is the contrast between the world's lies about you and God's truth about you:

> ➤ The world says: You are still a sinner because you sometimes sin. *God says: You are my saint who sometimes sins.*

> ➤ The world says: You get your identity from what you have done. *God says: You get your identity from what I have done for you.*

> ➤ The world says: You get your identity from what people say about you. *God says: You get your identity from what I say about you.*

> ➤ The world says: Your behavior tells you what to believe about yourself. *God says: Your belief about yourself directs your behavior.*

How you see yourself directs how you live out your faith walk—whether your faith walk will be a joyful one or not.

Songwriter Lauren Daigle captured this well in her song, "You Say."

> I keep fighting voices in my mind that say I'm not enough
> Every single lie that tells me I will never measure up
> Am I more than just the sum of every high and every low
> **Remind me** once again just **who I am because I need to know**
> The only thing that **matters now is everything You think of me**
> **In You I find my worth, in You I find my identity**
> You say I am loved when I can't feel a thing
> You say I am strong when I think I am weak
> And you say I am held when I am falling short
> And when I don't belong, oh **You say I am Yours**
> And **I believe What You say of me** Oh, I believe
> (Lauren Daigle, "You Say")

You need to believe what God says about you.

You have one secure, eternal answer to the identity question. By your faith in Jesus Christ, you can say, "I am in Christ, a dearly loved child of God, completely forgiven, and totally accepted by God"—an identity that no circumstance can change!

Grasping who you are in Christ is the third pathway to joy.

> *Write a short description of your identity in Christ based on what you discovered in the verses you read in this lesson. "I _____ (your name) am in Christ…"*

See a longer list of your identity characteristics at the end of this study guide (pages 111-114). You can make your own identity card (see page 114).

GRASPING YOUR IDENTITY SETS YOU FREE

Recommended: Listen to the podcast *"GRASPING YOUR IDENTITY SETS YOU FREE."* Use the section below as a listener guide.

You need to know who you are as a Christian.

> *So from now on we regard no one from a **worldly point of view**. Though we once regarded Christ in this way, we do so no longer. Therefore, if anyone is in Christ, **the new creation has come: The old has gone**, the new is here! (2 Corinthians 5:16-17)*

If you are in Christ, that means you have trusted in Christ as your Savior. From that very moment, you are made a new creation and given a new identity. And there are wonderful perks to discover about your new position in life. You need to know who you are as a Christian.

You are set apart from the world as God's saint.

> *Paul, a servant of Christ Jesus, called to be an apostle and **set apart** for the gospel of God... And you also are among those ... who are called to **belong to Jesus Christ**. To all ... who are loved by God and called to be his holy people... (Romans 1:1, 6-7)*

When Paul wrote that he was set apart, the word he used there means to be set apart from the world and dedicated to God for His purposes. That is an identity change.

Then, Paul went on to say that every believer likewise belongs to Jesus Christ, not to the world. Belonging to Jesus Christ means you are loved by God and called to be one of His saints. Other translations use the word "holy people." The Greek word used there means that you and I are set apart from sin and everything we had in the world before Christ. We are now dedicated to God for His purposes. Every Christian is one of God's saints. You and I are no longer common, ordinary human beings. We have a new identity.

You are set free to live a radically new kind of life.

Romans 3-5 describe how our faith in Jesus Christ sets us free from our previous sin-stained existence to enjoy a new life. God also knew that our ability to live out this freedom depends upon our understanding of who we are as believers in Jesus Christ. So He directed Paul's writing.

Throughout the letter to the Romans, Paul asked and answered questions he anticipated his readers were thinking. Romans 6 starts with this question, "Shall we go on sinning so that grace may increase?" In other words, if our sinfulness makes God's grace look so wonderful, then why not go on sinning so God can dish out more grace? Won't that make Him look good?" Paul's answer in Romans 6:1-3 could be put this way, "To think that way is ridiculous and illogical. Don't you know who you are?"

The New Testament teaches that believers in Jesus Christ get a new life with a radical new identity, something we never had before. No one before Jesus' resurrection ever had this new identity! Do you realize that? And this new identity **sets us free** to live a radically new kind of life, a joyful life. But not knowing our identity **enslaves** us to shoddy thinking and behavior, robbing us of our joy.

Not knowing your identity enslaves you.

Most Christians throughout the past 1700 years or so mainly knew they could have their sins forgiven and go to heaven when they died. And even then, they were not sure of that. The information about who they were as believers got lost in two things:

1) Illiteracy of the Bible through a lack of education and knowledge of what it actually says, and

2) Bondage to the poor teaching that one has to live by the church's rules to maintain God's acceptance—any church.

About 500 years ago, Martin Luther and other faithful believers who followed him rediscovered this identity treasure by reading and studying the Scriptures. After about 300 years, that teaching was replaced once again by emphasis on just getting your sins forgiven so you could go to heaven when you die with the addition that you had to live by certain "rules" to maintain that salvation. People were in bondage once again to illiteracy of the Bible and poor teaching.

The last fifty years have seen a Grace Awakening. Teaching about our new identity in Christ is everywhere in bookstores, on the radio, and on the internet. Yet, many believers still have no idea what their new identity is and all the benefits that come with it. Do you? Could you list them off the top of your head? And if you and I do not know who we are, how will we know that we have been **set free** to live a different kind of life?

Identity drives everything about life—especially spiritual life. Just saying, "I am a Christian" does not communicate much to you or anyone else if you do not know what it means.

How you see yourself directs how you live out your faith walk. You must know your identity. You can know your identity in Christ. And knowing your identity **sets you free**. Do you want to be free?

Knowing your identity sets you free.

Then, let us begin by knowing who you are. First and foremost, you are **in Christ**. The Bible tells us 130 times that believers are "in Christ." That must be pretty significant. What does that mean?

You learned in the lesson that from God's point of view, there are two kinds of people in the world —those who are in Adam and those who are in Christ. There is no middle ground. Who you are "IN" determines your identity and your options for living.

Everyone born on the planet is born in Adam. We inherited his sin nature. Sin is somewhere in our DNA. Scientists have not found the gene for it, but it is there. If someone ever found it, I am sure many of us would sign up for elective surgery. Get that thing out of there!

You were born in Adam. But now you are in Christ. How did that happen? Jesus died for your sin, and the Bible says that by your faith you died with Him. But there is more…

You are "dyed" with Christ.

> Or don't you know that all of us who were baptized into Christ
> Jesus were baptized into his **death**? We were therefore buried with
> him through baptism into **death**…. (Romans 6:3-4)

The Greek word translated "baptized" or "baptism" came from the process for "dyeing" cloth. For us, the Spirit does the dyeing—with Jesus—not with water or a color. Water baptism is a picture of what the Spirit does to us, but there is no mention of water in this passage. According to Acts 1:5, John baptized with water, but Jesus baptizes with the Holy Spirit. That is much more significant with far greater effects.

When you believed in Jesus Christ as your Savior, you were immediately baptized into Christ. You were "dyed" with Christ. When God looks on you and on me, He sees Jesus. We have been "dyed" with Christ. But wait, there is more!

You are "fused" with Christ.

> For if we have been **united** with him in a death like his, we will certainly also be **united** with him in a resurrection like his. *(Romans 6:5)*

The Greek word translated "united" literally means, "to make to grow together, to fuse." Being united with Christ, therefore, means that you become *fused together with Him*. Fusing items together creates something stronger and thicker than the original items. We are fused with Christ. That cannot be undone.

At your moment of fusing with Christ, you are no longer on your own, but Jesus' transforming life-giving power now lives in you. You are now connected to the King who has supreme power and authority. Your life is stronger and fulfills a greater purpose than what you could have done before the fusing. John Wesley, the 18th century preacher, said this, "Never think of yourself apart from Christ." You are continually **fused together** with Him and can live to enjoy the benefits of being in Him.

Make a fist with one hand to represent you. Now cover that fist with your other hand to represent Christ. You are "in Christ." That is who you are.

You can live to enjoy the benefits of being in Him.

The moment you believed, the old self that was born **in Adam** died. A new self with the same body but a new interior started life as a new person with a new nature and a new inheritance. This radical new identity means you can never go back to being in Adam. You will always be **in Christ.** Always!

God gives you a new nature and new inheritance because of His love for you.

What God does to give you and me a new identity with all these wonderful benefits is His choice, not ours. They are unconditional. They are God's gifts based on His love for you. The burden of performance is upon God—not on me, not on you. That is why knowing this is the pathway to a joyful walk. And if you have responded to God's grace and have a relationship with Him through faith in Jesus Christ, you are not who you used to be, either.

Does that give you joy?

God commits Himself to make your life match who you are in Christ.

No matter how long I have been walking with the Lord, in lots of ways my behavior and thoughts just do not look like Jesus. I bet yours do not, either. God knows this about us. That is why we need to understand His promise in Philippians.

> *...being confident of this, that he who began a good work in you will carry it on to completion until the day of Christ Jesus. (Philippians 1:6)*

God commits Himself to complete His work. Jesus' transforming power in you is continually working to match up your daily life with who you are, with what God sees when He looks at you in Christ. That is His part. What is your part?

You have a part in making your life match who you are in Christ.

(1) Know and believe who you are by faith, even when you cannot see it in yourself. That is the "how you see yourself" part.

(2) Yield to Jesus' transforming power working in you. That is the "how you live it out" part. We will cover that in the next lesson.

Let Jesus satisfy your heart with joy so that your daily walk with Him will be a joyful one.

Reflect

How you see yourself will influence how you think and live. Do you consider who you are in God's eyes (being in Christ) more than what the world thinks of you or what you think of yourself? Reflect on how the way you see yourself (past and present) influences your life.

Pray: Ask the Lord to help you see yourself as He sees you and to help you grasp the absolutely amazing gift of your new identity in Jesus Christ.

Choose Whom You Will Serve

But now that you have been set free from sin and have become slaves of God, the benefit you reap leads to holiness, and the result is eternal life. (Romans 6:22)

Pray: Lord Jesus, please teach me through this lesson.

PATHWAY #4

Think about a walk you chose to take that brings the word "misery" to mind. You wish you had never taken it.

What made it so miserable? Why did you choose to take it? Was there a better one you could have chosen instead?

We can get so busy with life that we neglect to think about the consequences of our choices. If you do not check the forecast before taking that 2-mile walk, you could get stuck in a storm. When you are hiking without a map and come across 2 trails, you could take the wrong trail and end up in a different location than planned. Choices have consequences.

You learned from Pathway #3 that your new identity in Christ sets you free to live a radically different kind of life with a new relationship between you and Jesus. You are dead to the old "you" that was controlled by sin and alive to the new "you" in Christ. You are on the right path, and it is looking pretty good. But the old "you" is still hanging around, trying to distract you away from serving Jesus. Choosing to serve your old self will lead to misery. **Pathway #4 is "Choose Whom You Will Serve."** The first steps along this pathway involve understanding your changed relationship to sin.

LIVING BY THE FLESH

While we as redeemed and justified believers have new life in Christ, we retain our old bodies in which sin dwells. The Bible calls this "the flesh." The term "flesh" (NIV: "sinful nature") refers to the portion of our humanity—our body, mind, emotions, and will through which indwelling sin assaults us. The flesh sends messages to the mind that demand a response. And our flesh is influenced by the world around us.

Read 1 John 2:16.

What are three areas of life influenced by the world?

Read Galatians 5:16-17.

How does Paul describe what you experience (verse 17)?

The flesh is in constant conflict with the Spirit. That conflict is fed by the lust of the flesh, the lust of the eyes, and the pride of life. This opposition is with us every day. That is why we must recognize the signals that our flesh gives us and make the choice every day how to live. The bad news is that the flesh does not improve or change its nature over time as long as we are in our bodies! At the moment of salvation, we are born again of the Spirit. Our bodies are **not** born again, and our mind, emotions, and will are **not** instantly transformed. The flesh does not improve, but the good news is that our choices can change over time as we learn to live by the Spirit instead. Living by the flesh is sin.

In Romans 6, Paul personified sin as a power that enslaves us—a slave master. Nearly 50% of people in the Roman Empire were slaves. Being set free would be like dying to that old slave master and being given a new life to live. That is what Paul described in Romans 6.

Read Romans 6:6-14.

Why was your old self crucified with Christ (verse 6)?

How should you think of yourself now (verses 7 and 11)?

What choices must you make as one dead to sin but alive to Christ (verses 12-13)?

Every human is born into bondage to the slave master sin. It does not matter how much money or status you have. It does not matter about your skin color or family history. You were born into bondage. You have a master and are a servant to something—either God and His righteousness or sin and its wickedness. There is no neutral ground. You might think you are your own master, but you are not! Self is really following the voice of master sin (the flesh) within you.

The rest of Romans chapter 6 reveals that there are choices to make. Your identity and all those benefits that God gives to you are His choice. How you let Him work in your life is your choice.

Read Romans 6:15-18.

What are your two choices (verse 16)?

What are you free to do now (verses 17 and 18)?

Read Romans 8:5.

What are your two choices?

All of your life before Christ, the old slave master sin called the shots. When you believed in Jesus, **a greater power moved in**—the Holy Spirit. He **sets you free from the power** of that old slave master to become what God intended you to be. But you are not set free to be your own master. That is not what it means to be set free. Your options are still to serve sin or to serve God.

You are dead to sin, but sin has not died to you. That old slave master is present in you until the day you leave your mortal body. It does not reform or go to sleep at any time. In fact, it yells pretty loudly sometimes. Yet, you do not have to listen or carry out its orders. You are freed from sin's power over you because a greater power lives in you who woos you to do right. You have a new master, Jesus Christ, who set you free.

You can choose to serve Christ by not letting sin reign in your mortal body to obey it. That means you do not offer parts of your body to sin as instruments of wickedness. Instead, offer every part of your body to God as instruments of righteousness, and recognize that sin is no longer your master as it once was. Realize that you got nothing good out of wickedness and see that you get great benefits from righteous living.

Read Galatians 5:19-26.

What are some evidences of living by the flesh (verses 19-21 and 26)?

What are evidences of living by the Spirit (verses 22-23)?

Often, we blame people or circumstances for our anger. People and circumstances do not cause our anger, impatience, or bitterness. Our reactions to people and circumstances reveal how we are living—by the Spirit or by the flesh.

Sin is obvious. The New Testament writers gave us plenty of descriptions of what sin looks like in a Christian's life! Just look at Mark 7, Ephesians 4 and 5, and Colossians 3. Living by the flesh is ugly! There is a stark contrast between the two lifestyles. Thanks be to God we are not left helpless like a pawn in the midst of the conflict. God acted to free us from sin's power and help us win the battle over sin. Thank you, Lord Jesus!

You and I are freed from sin's power in two ways:

(1) **Sin no longer makes you guilty before God and separated from Him.** We covered this in Pathways 2 and 3. Because of Christ's finished work on the cross and your faith in Him, God's anger against sin was satisfied. He is no longer angry at you, dear believer, because of your sin.

    The barrier of sin has been taken away. Your relationship with God is restored and is no longer broken. Your sin was transferred to Jesus Christ and taken away from you so that you are now completely forgiven and no longer burdened by your sin and guilt. You are declared not guilty and even righteous in God's sight. To God, you are perfected and no longer flawed by your sin.

    All of that is part of your identity in Christ. You need to know it and live with confidence in these truths.

(2) **A greater power has moved in—Jesus' transforming power.** God Himself through His Spirit is living inside your spirit. His presence inside you is why you can live a different kind of life.

LIVING BY THE SPIRIT

Living by the Spirit is a new way of living for any human. Before Christ, you did not have that option. You lived according to the flesh. After trusting in Christ, you are free to choose a new way of living—Spirit-led life. It is a much better way!

The Holy Spirit is **God Himself**, possessing all the divine attributes. He is a **Person**, not a "force" or merely an impersonal attribute or influence of God. The concept of the Holy Spirit's existence may seem like science fiction to you. We often feel this way because His name is more like a title. We have God the Father (we can relate to "father") and God the Son (whose name is Jesus, we can relate to "son" and "Jesus"). Paul often refers to the Spirit as the Spirit of Christ or God's Spirit to help us relate to Him.

The Holy Spirit is God's empowering presence in your life.

Read Titus 3:4-6.

What does the Spirit do for you (verse 5)?

Read John 14:15-20.

What did Jesus promise about the Spirit (verses 16-17)?

Read 1 Corinthians 2:12.

What is another benefit of receiving the Spirit?

Read Ephesians 3:16-21.

What does the Spirit do for you according to verse 16?

What does the Spirit do for you according to verse 20?

At the moment of salvation, the Holy Spirit enacts rebirth and renewal to every new believer. In other words, you were born again and given life (regeneration). The Spirit comes to live inside you representing Christ to you. In essence, Christ lives in you through the Spirit.

From the beginning of your faith relationship with Jesus Christ, the Holy Spirit anoints you with God's presence and power. You need both to live the kind of life Jesus intends for you to live. Once inside of you, He has an ongoing empowering ministry in your life. He teaches you what Jesus wants you to know and helps you understand what belongs to you as a saved one. He gives you power from the inside out to do what pleases God. His power in you is greater than your flesh and greater than the old slave master sin.

THE PATHWAY TO JOY

As a Christian, you are set free from sin's power in your life because you have God's Spirit—God's empowering presence in your life. And this great power, which can do more than we ask or imagine, is **at work within you** to do the work God wants done in your life.

But as you have learned in this lesson, you must choose to serve Jesus Christ with your body, mind, thoughts, tongue, fingers, and behavior. That is choosing to serve Jesus rather than submitting to your flesh. That choice requires recognizing what does not please Christ as your master and desiring what does please Him.

Read Romans 13:14.

What are your choices?

The Bible does not teach that if you live by the Spirit, the desires of the flesh will go away. As long as you live in your earthly body, sin remains a source of temptation in you. You can make the choice to not gratify the desires of the flesh but to clothe yourself with Christ as your master and depend on the Spirit to help you follow through with this choice. As Paul wrote in Romans 13, do not even think about how to gratify the desires of the flesh!

Choosing to serve Jesus is the fourth pathway to joy.

Is there some area of your life right now where you are listening to the wrong master? How will you apply the truth of this lesson to that area?

Consider saying this: "I am trusting Jesus to set me free from

_____

which is holding me in bondage."

For more information about the Holy Spirit's work in you, see "The Holy Spirit's Empowering Presence" in the resources at the end of this study guide (page 117).

CHOOSING TO SERVE JESUS

Recommended: Listen to the podcast "CHOOSING TO SERVE JESUS." Use the section below as a listener guide.

Jesus set you free! And out of gratitude, you should choose to serve the very One who did it. You can declare, "Lord Jesus, I am YOUR woman"—today, tomorrow, and the next day. But is that really possible? And are you willing to do that? What would it look like anyway?

Serve the one who set you free.

You need to understand your changed relationship to sin. Sin can no longer enslave you unwillingly because you have a super power in you—God Himself. You are continually being wooed to do what is right. When sin says, "Do this!" You can say, "No thanks. I don't need that. I am good." You have Holy Spirit super power in your heart to set you free to serve God instead of sin. He teaches you to say "No" to ungodliness and worldly passions (Titus 2:11-12). He reveals to you through the Word of God (the Bible) and through prayer what sins are in your life and helps your repentant heart follow through with your desire for change.

When your heart is open to Him, God helps you to recognize the temptations, and He gives you the way of escape—not through yourself but through the Spirit's empowering presence within you (1 Corinthians 10:13). Whether or not you are presently tempted in a given area, you are capable of committing any sin mentioned in the Bible, given the right set of circumstances, time, and temptation.

The progression of sin

The progression toward sin may be like this:

- A received thought produces familiarity.

- Continued pondering leads to curiosity and loss of repugnance.

- Desires are generated to experiment, sometimes coming as a total surprise. The most dangerous are the ones that blindside you with a desire you did not even know you could have!

- Having tried the activity, the flesh can learn to like, and even grow dependent on, any sensual stimulus.

Here is the truth you need to know: We never outgrow our need to depend 100% upon Jesus Christ. Recognizing this should lead us to have compassion on one another (Galatians 6:1) and to not take risks with sinful behavior!

A habit is easier to maintain than it is to start. Faith can be a habit—a good habit. Make wise decisions to protect yourself. Desires of the flesh do not go away. But just like a fire, they can burn hot or burn down, depending on whether you are feeding them. Do not feed the fire. Protect yourself by making policy decisions ahead of time to keep your distance from what tempts you. I heard those called "pre-decisions." We can also continually pray, "Lord, protect me from myself!"

Martin Luther was the priest who initiated the Protestant Reformation in the 1500s. He described it this way, "I cannot keep the birds from flying around my head; but by the grace of God I can keep them from building nests in my hair." What pre-decisions are you making or should you make ahead of time to protect yourself from what tempts you?

In Christ, you have options for living you never had before knowing Him. And you are free to choose daily to serve sin or to say, "Lord Jesus, I am YOUR woman today." That requires you to make up your mind. No person can serve two masters. You and I know the old slave master does not stop calling our names. Jesus says you have no obligation whatsoever to listen to sin. So let us look at your two options:

Option #1: Actively serve your new master Jesus.

What would that look like as a life decision? You would see yourself as fused with Christ. You would see sin as awful. You would commit yourself to being Jesus' woman every day. You would make the daily choice to submit to the Spirit's transforming power in you to make you more like Christ.

Because of your faith in Christ, God does not hold your sin against you any longer, and His grace is continually forgiving you of sin. But do not be deceived. That does not give you permission to intentionally sin. Intentional sin does not fit with who you are as a forgiven Christian with a new life to enjoy.

Yet, old habits die hard. As long as we live in these earthly bodies, we will be tempted to sin. Sin will happen—whether intentionally or unintentionally. So as an already forgiven Christian, you might ask, "How do I deal with sin when I recognize it in my life?" That is a great question.

Here is the biblical process for any believer to deal with recognized sin:

Step One: View yourself rightly.

Your identity is not "_____" (coveter, greedy, gossiper, whatever that sin is). You are in Christ, a child of God, who sometimes "____" (covets, is greedy, gossips...).

Step Two: Recognize the truth regarding your sin (confession).

To **confess** biblically means *to agree with God about what you and He both know to be true.* Confession is not a formula, a process, or dependent on a mediator. Regarding sin in your life, it is not saying, "I am sorry." It is saying, "I agree with you, God. I blew it!" You see your sin as something awful!

Using sexual immorality as an example: while reading 1 Thessalonians 4:1-8, the Spirit convicts you that sexual immorality in any form is not pleasing to God. God says to "flee/avoid immorality." You recognize this sin in your life. You agree with God that your immoral sexual behavior does not fit someone who knows God. That is confession.

Step Three: Confession is incomplete without repentance.

Repentance means *to change your mind about that sin, to turn away from it, to mourn its ugliness, resulting in changing your actions.* Paul said in 2 Corinthians 7:9-11 that godly sorrow brings repentance. It is saying, "I recognize what I am doing is wrong. This fills me with sorrow because it hurts You, God. Please help me to live differently." And that is how our lives get transformed.

For sexual immorality: You want to live in order to please God, and God wants you to avoid sexual immorality. So you pray, "Lord Jesus, please have your Spirit nudge me when I am not holy and honorable with my body. Help me to say no to temptation and to give up any relationship that is not honorable to you. By faith, Lord, I want you to do that in my life." That is repentance.

Repentance is not repentance until you change something. You can confess "until the cows come home" (daily, habitually) and never change anything. Jesus called for people to "repent" not to just "confess."

Step Four: Repentance leads to dependence.

Depend on the living Christ inside you for change to take place. Our Lord Jesus Christ is not interested in our compliance or outward conformity as much as He desires our **obedience from the heart.**

For sexual immorality: Memorize 1 Thessalonians 4:3-8 and any other scriptures that deal with staying pure and not rejecting God's instructions. Be sensitive to the Spirit's nudging when you are tempted to do otherwise. Desire a life that pleases God and make pre-decisions not to be sexually impure. It is okay to say, "Lord Jesus, I cannot do this on my own. I trust you to do this in me and through me." Then, watch what He does!

That is actively serving your new master Jesus.

> We have provided this tool, "The Biblical Process for Dealing with Recognized Sin," at the end of this study guide using "grumbling" as another example (page 95).

But what if you don't want to listen to the Spirit. What if you would rather hang onto your favorite sin? That is option #2.

Option #2: Be passive to your new master and say "yes" to the old master sin.

That might look like this:

- You think to yourself, "I am saved and going to heaven when I die. So I don't think I have a problem with that sin." That makes the old slave master "Sin" perk up its ears.

- You don't acknowledge or care about your identity in Christ. You don't see how doing that sin affects Him.

- You refuse to acknowledge your sin even though your pastor or Bible Study makes you aware of it. It is more fun to keep doing it, which makes the old slave master "Sin" just smile with glee.

- You don't want to change. So you don't ask the Spirit to nudge you when you are doing that behavior. Even if He does, you ignore Him. You are not interested in agreeing with Him. This makes the old slave master "Sin" laugh victoriously. Gotcha!

The result is you actually put yourself in bondage to THAT sin.

Note three things about choosing option #2:

(1) You are **not** free to choose when or how the consequences of that sinful behavior will hurt you or those you love. Living passively to God or pursuing a sinful lifestyle as a believer does not change your identity. But it does change your usefulness to God and

definitely the enjoyment of your benefits in Christ. You are not going to have a joyful walk.

(2) You are **not** free to stop the Holy Spirit's work in you to make you like Jesus—the easy way or the hard way. And He will!

(3) You **are** free to finally come to your senses, agree with God that you have been sinning deliberately, and allow Him to change your behavior to match your identity in Christ and what pleases Him. It is never too late to say, **"Lord Jesus, I am YOUR woman"** again.

Being passive to your new master Christ and saying yes to the old slave master "Sin" is not your best option, is it?

Actively serving Jesus as your master is your best option.

Actively serve Jesus. Yet, even while actively serving Him, you may be trusting Him with some aspects of your life while not doing so in others. Over a lifetime, the Lord reveals areas of your life that you need to surrender to Him. When you do so, the greater power within you—God Himself—changes you. You experience being set free from the power of sin in that area of your life. This is the best lifestyle to choose.

Choose to say this with me, "Lord Jesus, I am YOUR woman today." Will you say that tomorrow and the day after that?

Let Jesus satisfy your heart with joy so that your daily walk with Him will be a joyful one.

Reflect

Read Psalm 139:23-24.

> *Reflect on the heart attitude you need to stay faithful to Christ as your master.*

Pray: Ask Jesus to show you where you are serving sin instead of Him. Repent of that sin and depend on Him to help you make needed changes in your life.

Claim Your Freedom in Christ

It is for freedom that Christ has set us free. Stand firm, then, and do not let yourselves be burdened again by a yoke of slavery. (Galatians 5:1)

Pray: Lord Jesus, please teach me through this lesson.

PATHWAY #5

Think about a walk you have taken (or could take) with people who criticize everything you do because you do not do it right according to them. Your pace is too slow or too fast. You are not wearing the right kind of shoes or clothes.

How would you feel? What might you long to do?

Such a walk would likely be miserable. You might feel stuck on that walk and captive to your companions until you could get free from them. That can happen to you in your spiritual life as well.

Many Christians start out accepting the gift of salvation by grace. Then, others impose on them things they must "do" or "not do." It is communicated as "follow our rules" in order to *maintain your acceptance before a holy God*. This may have been your experience. This issue is called "law and grace." The false teaching is called legalism. The way out of legalism is **Pathway #5: "Claim Your Freedom in Christ."**

LAW AND GRACE

When you hear the word "legalism," you probably think "legal" which deals with laws and rules. The Jews followed "the Law" consisting of over 600 commands given by God only to the nation of Israel. The 600+

commands are found in the books of Exodus and Leviticus and showed the Jewish people how to live holy lives in the land God gave to them where He also dwelled with them. The religious rules found in the Jewish Law were fulfilled in Christ and have been replaced by a new way of approaching life—living by the Spirit. You learned about that in the last lesson *(Pathway #4: Choose Whom You Will Serve)*.

In the New Testament, Christians were being pushed into following the Jewish Law in some form. Today, it is not likely that you will be pushed into following the Jewish Law, although some Christian groups add parts of it to their own religious practices. You are more likely to run into the legalism that is a performance-based way of approaching the Christian life.

Answer the following questions for yourself to see how much you have been influenced by a works-related way of living out your Christian life.

1. Is your motivation to live the Christian life and please God based on fear of what God will do to you every time you fail? Or is it based on love and gratitude for what Christ has done for you?

2. Do you try to motivate others to obedience through fear of punishment—given out by God or by you? Or do you recognize the grace God has shown you so you encourage others to obedience out of hearts of love and gratitude to Him?

3. Do you think the power to live the Christian life is through self-effort (trying hard enough)? Or is it Spirit-empowered (trusting in the Spirit to enable you to do so)?

Probably the simplest way to understand "law & grace" is to see it as the issue of God's acceptance: "On what basis are you made acceptable to a holy God?"

> *Based upon what you have learned so far in your faith walk or in this book, how would you answer that question?*

The bondage of legalism

God's plan is too easy for many to accept. And old habits of works-based religion are hard to break. As seen in New Testament writings, false teachers called "Judaizers" began telling the new Gentile Christians that they had to become Jews first, get circumcised, and start obeying the Mosaic Law in order to be acceptable to God and receive salvation through faith in Christ. As you would expect, this stirred up a lot of controversy in the early church.

News reached Paul about this false teaching that messed with the minds and hearts of the new believers in the Galatian churches. With firmness and clarity, Paul wrote a letter to the Galatians to address the panic created by the Judaizers' teaching. Yet, the warnings and truths are applicable to anyone today who has been taught you must do certain works to maintain your salvation and acceptance by God.

Read Galatians 1:6-7.

Who and what were the Galatians deserting?

Read Galatians 3:1-3.

After beginning by means of the Spirit, what are they doing now (verse 3)?

Read Galatians 5:1.

Christ has set them free. To enjoy that freedom, what should they not do?

When you turn to legalism, you are deserting Christ! The gospel message is His. We receive all the benefits of our salvation by His grace, not through any works of our own (Ephesians 2:8-9). God does the work in us through His Spirit. The Galatians had begun their faith walk by the Spirit who gave them new life and a new identity in Christ. Now, they were trying to finish by human effort, putting themselves in a yoke of slavery to all the rules and regulations of the Mosaic Law. As Peter said in Acts 15:10, "Why do you try to test God by putting on the necks of Gentiles a yoke that neither we nor our ancestors have been able to bear?" Paul agreed with Peter and with God. Don't let anyone put you in that bondage again. Instead, live in your freedom through the Spirit. Live out your life based on grace. What happened back then is still with us today.

The danger of legalism

Legalism **is the addition of any other conditions to faith in Christ in order to gain and maintain acceptance from God,** and even how to stay saved. It is taking your faith in Christ and adding other things you must do or not do for God to accept you and let you keep your salvation. You can recognize it as "faith plus good works" or "faith plus following church rules" or "faith plus not **that** sin."

> *Do you recognize the influence of "faith plus _____"*
> *teachings in your life so you would remain acceptable to God?*

Legalism is not a reference to what is clearly taught in the New Testament about what sin is and what living a life that pleases God looks like (what you learned in Pathway #4). Legalism consists of those extra rules that some person or organization has decided you must follow to be a "good Christian" and for God to really love you.

Read Colossians 2:16-23.

> *Do not let anyone judge you by what (verse 16)?*

Those religious rituals pointed to what Christ has now accomplished for all people (verse 17). No one needs to abide by them any longer.

When you start following other ways to "be spiritual," you are deserting whom as Lord of your life (verse 19)? See also Colossians 1:15-18.

Do not submit to what legalistic commands (verses 21-22)?

Such legalistic commands have an appearance of wisdom but lack value at doing what (end of verse 23)?

The Bible teaches you to not let anyone impose religious practices on you that Christ has not commanded you to do (what you eat or drink, participation in religious festivals, and Sabbath requirements). Seeking "spiritual experiences" can lead to pride (being puffed up) and disconnection from the supremacy of Christ as your Head. Restrictions on what you can handle, taste, or touch lead to an appearance of wisdom but lack any value in controlling sinful lusts of the flesh.

Modern examples of legalism are rules that say you can listen to only certain kinds of music and not wear certain types of clothing. Legalism makes rules for when and how often you must attend church and what you are allowed to eat and drink to stay acceptable to God. Legalism declares certain activities sinful when God does not. Legalism also includes denying yourself the normal activities and pleasures of life in order to make yourself look good or earn merit with God by what you "sacrifice." Following such checklists can cause boasting and a hardened heart toward others who do not abide by such rules.

Legalism includes following the Jewish Law, human "religious" laws imposed by others, or self-imposed rules that you feel make you more spiritual than others. The effects on the individual of any living by works are the same—fear, guilt, and condemnation. You know you are trapped in legalism whenever you try **to approach God on the basis of your own merits or performance.** Your focus is drawn away from the Person of Jesus Christ and His finished work on the cross (Galatians 1:6; Colossians 2:19). Instead of enjoying a relationship with Him, you are practicing a religion. This is opposite of God's plan for you.

Read Ephesians 2:8-9.

Why did God choose to give you salvation by His grace based on your faith alone and not by your works (end of verse 9)?

LIVING BY GRACE

Why do some Christians so easily stray away from grace into legalism? Often, it is because of the fear of lawlessness. Lawlessness is wrong and should be opposed. The temptation is to think that sin can be controlled through lots of rules. We all know how much that does not work! Trying to control sin through rules that God does not even give us does not work. The answer is to teach and exhort every Christian to "live by the Spirit"—the better way.

Read Romans 5:8.

Why should you want to obey God with your life?

Read Ephesians 2:4-5.

Why should you want to obey God with your life?

Read 2 Corinthians 5:14-15.

Why should you want to obey God with your life?

Read Galatians 2:20.

Why should you want to obey God with your life?

The answer to each question above can simply be GRATITUDE for God's great LOVE for you. God loves you and demonstrated that love through Christ's death on the cross. Christ's love compels you to live for Him because of what He did for you. As you have learned in this study, you have a new identity and status through your faith in Christ. You have the Holy Spirit to lead you and change you from the inside out.

Read Colossians 1:29.

Are you supposed to live the Christian life by your self-effort or by Christ's power in you?

Read Titus 2:11-14.

Grace teaches you to say "no" to ungodliness and worldly passions and to do what instead (verse 12, second part)?

What is Christ's goal (verse 14)?

The Christian life is to be lived by faith in Christ who is living in you. You should yield your will to His work in you to work out His purpose in your life. The work of Christ's super power in you is greater than your self-effort. You are NOT left to be as good as you can be on your own!

Grace motivates you to obey God out of love and gratitude for what Christ has done. You want to live a life that pleases Him.

THE PATHWAY TO JOY

Go back to the three questions we asked at the beginning of this lesson.

1. If your **motivation** to live the Christian life and please God is based on fear of what God will do to you every time you fail, delete that from your brain. You are a dearly loved child of God who completely forgives you for every sin. Bask in God's grace for you and let your love and gratitude for what Christ has done for you be your motivation to live a life that pleases Him.

2. If you think that you can **motivate** others to obedience through fear of punishment—given out by God or by you, you will only contribute to hardening their hearts toward you and toward God. You probably know people who were raised in legalism who now want nothing to do with a God who can never be pleased. Claim the grace God has shown you so you can encourage others to obedience out of hearts of love and gratitude as well.

3. If you think the **power** to live the Christian life is through self-effort (trying hard enough), you are attached to a losing cause. You can never be good enough to please God through your own efforts, no matter how hard you try. That is why Christ died on the cross for you. Your life as a believer is now Spirit-empowered. You can trust in the Spirit to enable you to live a life that pleases the Lord.

Living by faith is acting according to the Word of God, depending on Jesus Christ for the power, and trusting Him with the results. As you learn from your study of God's word, you will see the kind of life that God desires for you to have—thoughts and behaviors that are pleasing to Him. As He shows you where you need to change something in your life, you can say this, *"Lord Jesus, I cannot do this on my own. But you can do this in me. I want you to do this in my life. I trust you to do this in my life."* Then, watch what He does!

Claiming your freedom from the bondage of legalism is the fifth pathway to joy.

What has Christ revealed to you in this lesson about your motivation to live a Christian life? Consider how any legalism has affected your life, emotions, thinking, or relationship with God and others. Ask the Lord Jesus to help you let it go and cling to the truth of your identity in Christ and the grace of God for you.

For a more detailed study of the law and grace issue, get the "Graceful Living" Bible Study by Melanie Newton.

PURSUING GODLINESS TO AVOID LEGALISM

Recommended: *Listen to the podcast "PURSUING GODLINESS TO AVOID LEGALISM." Use the section below as a listener guide.*

Godliness is devotion to God expressed in a life that is pleasing to Him.

Devotion to God begins with loving Him so much that you want to please Him with your life. The New Testament is filled with reasons why you should devote yourself to God and love Him wholeheartedly. That devotion should be expressed in a response of obedience to Him—a response motivated by love and gratitude. Sadly, you can be taught instead that you must do certain works to keep your salvation and avoid certain activities in order not to lose it. You can recognize it as "faith plus good works" or "faith plus following church rules."

Legalism is not what is clearly taught in the New Testament about what sin is and what living a life that pleases God looks like. Legalism is someone trying to motivate you to live the Christian life based on your own efforts and fear of what God will do to you every time you fail. That is the end result of legalism. It is very wrong and destructive!

Legalism denies Christ's finished work on the cross.

To claim your freedom, you need to know that legalism denies Christ's finished work on the cross on your behalf. The gospel is an announcement to the world of an accomplished fact. What God set out to do for humans, He accomplished. The apostles declared this from the time of Pentecost (Acts 2) and beyond.

Salvation is available on the basis of a single condition: faith. God acted. We are to respond to His action. Those who respond with faith in Jesus Christ, who is God's Son, receive a firm assurance of eternal security, a new identity in Christ, and a true knowledge of God as seen through all that He has done through Christ's finished work on the cross *(Pathway #3: Grasp Who You Are)*.

Because of Christ's finished work, you are **justified**. That means you are declared righteous and no longer guilty of your sin. You are **saved from the wrath of God**. That means that His anger against sin was satisfied by Jesus' death on the cross. He is no longer angry at your sin. You are **reconciled**. That means your relationship with God is restored and is no longer broken. You have direct and instantaneous access to Him. You are **redeemed**. That means you are released from wickedness and no longer in bondage to sin. You are completely **forgiven** and no longer burdened by your sin and guilt. You are **sanctified**. That means you are perfected in God's eyes (holy, without blemish, and free from accusation) and no longer flawed because of your sin. And God continues to work in your life so that your behavior will one day match how He sees you (Hebrews 10:14).

Legalism denies all the work that God has already accomplished on your behalf and makes rules that God does not command. Legalism demands you make yourself look good or earn merit with God by what you sacrifice. And if you cannot measure up to its expectations, legalism makes you feel guilt and shame, not gratitude and joy.

Do not let anyone take from you the truths of who you are in Christ. They are FACTS for every Christian, made yours the moment you put your faith in Christ. Claim Christ's finished work on the cross for you.

Legalism is not a substitute for godliness.

To claim your freedom, you also need to know that legalism is not a substitute for godliness. Often, when you examine the lives of those who push legalism on you, you will find that those people are some of the most ungodly in their private lives. Why is that?

Legalism feeds hypocrisy.

To His disciples, Jesus pointed out legalism in the Pharisees who kept their bodies squeaky clean while treating fellow Jews like dirt (Mark 7:18-23). Cleanliness is not next to godliness. What they did was hypocrisy. Hypocrisy comes from the word for "actor." It is playing a role.

Christians who make mistakes and repent of them before God are not hypocrites. No Christian is perfect in life—no matter how old or established in their faith.

Hypocrites are those who are outwardly conforming to what looks good (what you saw in the lesson), but their hearts are not tender toward God. They claim to know God, but by their actions they deny Him. *Titus 1:16*

God is not interested in outward conformity. He wants your heart to be right with Him, and right behavior that He asks you to do should follow that. But legalism feeds hypocrisy.

Legalism feeds hopelessness.

Many Christians start out accepting the gospel of God's grace by their faith alone. Then, someone comes along and says, "That is not enough. You have to follow these rules if you want to be spiritual and if you want to stay saved." But those rules are constantly changing so you never know if you are saved or not!

Maybe you started out accepting the gift of salvation by faith in Jesus as a free gift but then you were thrown into a "follow our rules" way of living this Christian life in order to maintain your acceptance before God. The result is that you stray away from enjoying a love-based relationship with Jesus to practicing a works-based religion. Jesus also addressed this in Matthew 23:2-4.

Outward performance is not godliness. But the emphasis on "getting it right" with God can lead to hopelessness because no one can ever please God enough through their own efforts. So you might just stop trying altogether and give up.

Legalism is used to motivate people to obedience by fear of punishment. In doing so, legalism becomes a substitute for devotion to Christ and true godliness that flows from that devotion.

God's plan is for you to live by grace.

Claim your freedom from legalism as you live by God's grace and in God's grace to you every day.

> *For it is by grace you have been saved, through faith—and this is not from yourselves, it is the gift of God—**not by works**, so that no one can boast. (Ephesians 2:8-9)*

Grace means "undeserved favor." God gives His favor to someone not because they are good enough to deserve it but because His love chooses to do so. We all receive this grace when we trust in Jesus.

God wants you to relate to Him now on the basis of His grace. Jesus paid the complete price for you to be set free from your sinful past. You can do nothing more to make yourself acceptable to God.

Paul understood those who had been relating to God through outward performance. It was part of his own story. (1 Timothy 1:13-14). God's overflowing grace sets you free from whatever has you in bondage—sin, guilt, religious expectations, whatever.

Grace should be what motivates you to obedience. Knowing what Christ has done for you should fill your heart with love and gratitude to Him so that you want to live the kind of life that pleases Him.

So we make it our goal to please him... (2 Corinthians 5:9)

You can make it your goal and actively pursue godliness—godlikeness—because you love Him and are thankful for what He has done for you. Remember your identity in Christ makes you perfectly and continually acceptable to God as His dearly loved child. Do not let anyone try to take that away from you!

Let Jesus satisfy your heart with joy so that your daily walk with Him will be a joyful one.

Reflect

God wants you to relate to him on the basis of His grace, so that your motivation to obey Him is based on His love for you, your love for Him, and gratitude for what Christ has done for you. Relax! And enjoy your grace-filled relationship with God today, tomorrow, and forever!

Respond to God with gratitude for the grace-filled life He has given you. Feel free to use any creative means to do so (poetry, prose, drawing, song). We have provided an extra page for you to use.

Pray: Thank God that you have freedom to relate to Him on the basis of His grace to you. Ask Him to help you recognize any legalism that has influenced your life and prevented you from having a joyful walk with Christ.

Keep Moving Forward

Consider it pure joy, my brothers and sisters, whenever you face trials of many kinds, because you know that the testing of your faith produces perseverance. Let perseverance finish its work so that you may be mature and complete, not lacking anything. (James 1:2-4)

Pray: Lord Jesus, please teach me through this lesson.

PATHWAY #6

Picture in your mind a walk you took that was very hard to do. Maybe you did not know how long it would take or how it would turn out. But at the end, you realized it was so worth it.

What made it hard? What made finishing it worth the trouble?

I remember a 6-hour, 4000-foot uphill hike with my husband in Colorado. It was cold and drizzly, and my body hurt all the way up. But I was rewarded at the end of that "suffering" with the most gorgeous display of wildflowers I had ever seen in a mountain-peak ringed area called Chicago Basin. I still have that feeling of awe when I think about it. Enduring the hike was so worth it!

In order to see that beautiful reward, I had to keep moving forward. That is **Pathway #6: "Keep Moving Forward."**

SUFFERING HAS A PURPOSE

Something is going on somewhere in your country, in your town, in your neighborhood, or in your family that has made someone upset, nervous, or in a panic mode—maybe even you. Cancer. Disaster. Job loss. Death. Enemy attack. For those of us who like to plan and control our environment so that our loved ones (and ourselves) can rest, relax, and be productive, these interruptions to life are very hard to bear. So we try to escape to something that makes it go away for a while—a feel-good movie, book, retreat, or some not-so-healthy things. But then we get back to the rough-and-tumble of real life and find that whatever is stressing us is still there. Most stressors do not last just for a day—more like a month or year or even a decade. Right?

Read John 16:33.

What will happen to everyone, even Jesus' followers?

Jesus said that all of us will have trouble in this world. It does not matter where you live or how much money you have or what kind of success you have gained. It does not even matter how much faith you have or how faithful you have been to God in your daily life and work.

Some troubles simply come from living in this fallen world and are common to everyone such as illness and natural disasters. Other troubles like persecution and rejection are related to being a child of God living in an unbelieving world. Then there are those we inflict upon ourselves because of sin still present within us—our own bad choices— or troubles that others inflict upon us because of their bad choices. Either way, we get stuck with the results. Maybe that is what you are experiencing right now.

Read Romans 5:1-5.

What good things do you have in Christ (verses 1-2)?

In what else are you to glory or rejoice (verse 3) and why?

Perseverance or endurance produces character and hope. (verse 4). Hope does not disappoint because of what (verse 5)?

How does that make you feel?

Those wonderful benefits (peace with God, being justified through faith, access to God's grace, and hope) are part of your identity in Christ *(Pathway #3: Grasp Who You Are)* and reasons for rejoicing. Then, suffering is thrown in with all that good stuff. The Bible says we can know that sufferings or troubles can produce something good in us— perseverance. Perseverance produces character which produces hope and experiencing God's love being poured out into our hearts.

Years earlier, the Holy Spirit inspired Jesus' half-brother James to write something similar:

Read James 1:2-4.

Write verse 2 in the space below.

Trials test your faith and produce what (verse 3)?

Perseverance or endurance works to make you what (verse 4)?

To "face" means to fall into the midst of something that surrounds you on all sides like a sinkhole. The only way out is for someone to pull you up from above. Pure joy is the deep, inner gladness that only comes from God through our faith in Christ. It is unpolluted by what is happening around you. And when James said "consider it pure joy," he was referring to an act of the will not the emotions.

If someone came up to you while you are suffering and said, "Find joy in your sufferings," how would you respond? If you are right now in the midst of something that seems awfully like a trial, you likely want some counsel that makes sense. So let us wrap our minds around what both Paul and James were thinking as the Holy Spirit inspired their writing.

PERSEVERANCE IS GOOD FOR US

As humans, we face all kinds of stress, pressure, and pain in just trying to survive physically, financially, or socially. That stress makes us more susceptible to compromise with sin to avoid the suffering. The Bible teaches us that in order to keep moving forward on a joyful walk with Christ, you and I need to have something called **perseverance**, something the Bible says is good for us. It is like the word "endurance" but more intentional.

The English word perseverance means *holding to a course of action, belief, or purpose without giving way.* Holding to—without giving way. In Romans and James, the Greek word translated "perseverance" also carries the idea of "bearing under." That implies some kind of weight.

So perseverance is holding up a load or long-term burden with staying power, tenacity, and stick-to-it-iveness. It carries the idea of whole life experience, not just getting stuck in traffic. It is the quality that enables a person to stand on his or her feet when facing a storm head on. And doing so makes you stronger just like load-bearing exercise makes your bones stronger. Nutrition alone will not develop strong bones. Bible study alone will not develop perseverance. Staying on your feet and moving forward in a storm does. Sadly, for those of us who are book learners, we cannot learn perseverance from a book. We only learn it by going through suffering. There has to be a challenge to our comfort. And who likes that?!

The Bible teaches that you need perseverance to keep moving forward with joy as you face suffering, trouble, or carry a long-term burden. Perseverance is necessary for every Christian's faith walk. And there is a reward at the end for persevering—character, hope, becoming mature and complete, not lacking anything. Do you want that? So where do you learn perseverance?

STAY FOCUSED ON JESUS

Read Hebrews 12:1-3.

To move forward with perseverance, you must what (verse 1)?

Your focus must stay where (verse 2)?

What example does He set for you (verse 2)?

Following His example helps you to do what (end of verse 3)?

The imagery used in verse 1 is that of a race in a great amphitheater filled with people. These are not spectators but witnesses who can offer testimony to you of the value of putting faith in God even when you cannot see the end. They lived that way. The witnesses are those listed by name or description in Hebrews chapter 11. **Their lives testified that perseverance is possible.** They persevered through many different challenging life circumstances.

The race is the rough-and-tumble of real life. It is not a Hallmark movie where everything is scripted to end sweetly. It is not a fantasy world where you have magical control over what happens. It is real life. Real life hurts. It is confusing. It blindsides us. When we are in the middle of that real life, some things keep us from moving forward with joy along a difficult pathway—hindrances and sin habits. We covered dealing with sin habits in *Pathway #4: Choose Whom You Will Serve*. Let us talk about hindrances here.

> *Consider personal things or choices that could hinder a runner from success in a race. What comes to mind?*

> *What things in your life are hindrances to your faith walk?*

For a runner, you might have thought about wearing the wrong clothes, the wrong shoes, not getting to the race on time, not getting nourished before or during the run, being distracted by other runners, not following the signs, or doing it alone. We often cling to similar things that hinder us—poor time management, getting distracted by other people, and neglecting proper nourishment. We have to make the choice to throw off everything that hinders us and move forward on our faith walk with perseverance, while fixing our eyes on Jesus.

"To fix" means to turn the eyes away from other things and fix them on one thing with attentiveness. Our focus is to be on Jesus as we move forward on our pathway. We are to fix our eyes on Jesus, not on the distractions that draw us away from Him.

> We are called first and foremost to a **Person** ... There is a striking parallel between the baby's dependent relationship with its mother and our life of dependency on Christ. Because of its dependent life, a baby in the womb could say, "For me, to live is Mom." In the same way, we can say, "For me, to live is Christ." (Bob George, *Growing in Grace*, p. 78)

Christianity is Christ. It is not a code of rules or an organization. It is a relationship with Him. When we stay focused on Jesus, we know we are not alone. He is with us, in us, and for us. We are being transformed along our walk to become more like Him. We have a Savior who has walked through life before us. He knows how hard it is. He knows how to persevere through it. We can trust Him.

We are not only to stay focused on Him but also to learn how to live dependently on Him as we persevere through any trouble in life.

LIVE DEPENDENTLY ON JESUS

Read 2 Corinthians 1:8-9.

What did Paul and his companions experience (verse 8)?

How did they feel about it (end of verse 8, first part of verse 9)?

What was God's purpose in letting them go through that trouble (end of verse 9)?

God's purpose is the same for you and me. In all of life, whether or not you are currently facing trouble, God wants you to learn to not depend on yourself but to depend on Him and His great power, which raised Jesus from the dead. He wants you to put your hope in Him and count on His work to give you what you need to face your troubles.

Read 2 Corinthians 12:7-10.

In the New Testament, "the Lord" refers to Jesus Christ. Three times, Paul asked Christ to take away one of his troubles (likely a physical ailment, verse 7).

> *What was Christ's answer to this man whom He loved dearly (verse 9, first part)?*

> *What was Paul's response to Christ's decision (verse 9, second part)?*

> *What was the result of that choice (verse 10)?*

Could you say that regarding your troubles and weaknesses?

The Lord did not take away one of the hurts that Paul was experiencing. He said that His grace to Paul was sufficient for Paul to manage any weakness because the Lord knew it drove Paul to rely upon Him more. Paul's response was to rejoice in anything that makes Christ stronger in him.

Remember that the best and most loving parents still must let their children hurt sometimes in order for them to live as adults (cutting teeth, learning to walk, gaining and losing friends). God loves you even more than the best parents could every day. He wants you to learn how to live as His child, depending on Him for the comfort and strength that flows from God's grace for you.

Human parents raise their children to be less dependent on them and more independent. God raises His children to be **less independent of Him and more dependent on Him**.

Whatever makes us rely on Him more is good for us, even if it hurts.

That feeds perseverance in your life. Perseverance is also fed by hope.

THE GIFT OF HOPE IN THIS DIFFICULT WORLD

In Romans 5, you read that perseverance leads to hope in your life. Biblical hope is not wishful thinking but *a confident, eager expectation of a coming certainty* based on the character of God to back up His promises. You can have hope because Jesus Christ is always with you. You can hold onto Him without giving way because He is holding onto you (John 10:28-29). And He has given us something else to feed our hope.

Read Romans 15:4-5.

What contributes to your hope (verse 4)?

When we look at life with just our own eyes, we can become fearful and pessimistic. We think to ourselves, "Nothing's going to work. I do not know if I can get through this." But when we look at the Bible and see how God empowered everyday people like you and I to face their challenges, the Holy Spirit uses that Scripture to strengthen and give us courage we did not know we had. His powerful presence in us will give us the perseverance we need to face any storm along our faith walk.

THE PATHWAY TO JOY

We live in the time period between Genesis 3 when sin entered the world and Revelation 21 when God does away with all sin and its effects. Where there is sin, there is decay, destruction, and death—relationally, emotionally, and physically. Hard stuff is going to happen to even the best of Jesus' followers. Jesus said so. James and Paul repeated it. This is foundational.

Other people may promise that if you just have enough faith, "Nothing bad should happen." Have you heard that? Is it possible? Yes. Is it reasonable? No! So when bad things do happen, you might be blown away or so disappointed that you give up on your faith-walk. But Jesus does not promise an easy time. He put it right out there in John 16:33 so we will know, *"in this world you will have trouble,"* trials of many kinds. Troubles are a normal and expected human experience. Then He said, *"But take heart! I have overcome the world."*

How could having perseverance help you on your faith walk?

Consider anything in your life that gets in the way of perseverance during trouble so you have difficulty moving forward. It is okay to say this, "Lord Jesus, I cannot handle this, but You can. I will trust you to help me to get rid of what hinders me. Please keep me moving forward in trusting you through this storm in my life." Then, watch what He does!

Asking for perseverance to keep moving forward is the sixth pathway to joy.

Reflect on the song lyrics below. Respond to God with a declaration of your own trust in Him to keep moving forward in the midst of your heartaches and troubles.

I know You're able and I know You can save through the fire with Your mighty hand. But even if You don't, my hope is You alone.
I know the sorrow, and I know the hurt would all go away if You'd just say the word. But even if You don't, my hope is You alone.

("Even If" by Mercy Me)

Get *"Profiles of Perseverance"* Bible Study by Melanie Newton for a more detailed study of perseverance.

ASKING FOR PERSEVERANCE TO MOVE FORWARD

Recommended: *Listen to the podcast "*ASKING FOR PERSEVERANCE TO MOVE FORWARD.*" Use the section below as a listener guide.*

Perseverance is holding to a course of action, belief, or purpose without giving way.

We develop perseverance through experience not through head knowledge.

God's method of teaching us perseverance

God's way of developing perseverance in our lives is this: "Prepare by instruction; learn by experience."

"Prepare by instruction" means studying the truths about God and His way of approaching life in the Bible. It also includes viewing God's work in the lives of men and women in the Bible during much of their lifetime. You can see God's faithfulness to them and be confident in His faithfulness to you as well. He is the same God.

"Learn by experience" means you trust in what you believe about God as you live out your life, and you apply what you learn from the Bible to every situation you face. It is being teachable. You can face any impossible situation if you are prepared by instruction from God and teachable to learn through experience with God. Perseverance is learned by experience.

Perseverance requires the testing of your faith.

Suffering tests your faith. You know that to be true. Perseverance through that suffering actually makes your faith more beautiful. Testing refers to the process of melting down rock called ore that has suspected gold in it. It is tested to see **how much** gold is in it and to remove anything that is not gold. Fire melts the ore. The heavier gold metal sinks. The weaker crud that is not gold floats to the top and is skimmed off, leaving just the real stuff. The gold in the ore was already gold before being melted. But after melting, all that is left of the ore is pure and is useful for making jewelry, money, and decorations. Valuable stuff.

The testing of your faith is on faith you actually have. That is one reason to rejoice. You have faith worth testing. Gold in any amount is beautiful.

Jesus uses those tough times, when you are under stress, pressure, pain, or suffering to float to the surface the parts of your character that are not so beautiful, not so strong, and not so godly. Those are the hindrances and entanglements that keep us from moving forward. And if we let Him, He will remove that not-so-beautiful stuff and strengthen what is left so we can **persevere.** The result is having stronger faith.

Here is what can happen, especially for those of us who became believers as adults. Old habits and ways of doing things are hard to forget or ignore. Maybe you have been a believer for only a few years and had twenty years or more experience living life the world's way, not God's way. So when tough times hit, you revert to what worked for mom, dad, or your friends. You might rely on what you see through social media, in movies, and on TV. When tough times hit, you keep your options open like this, "I will try my mom's way, then my friend's way, then God's way," and so forth.

That is sin. The scary thing is that if you choose to deal with the problem in a sinful way, Jesus will let you! We talked about that in *Pathway #4: Choose Whom You Will Serve.* But you are not going to get the wisdom to hold up. Are you double-minded like that? You know you are a Christian. You know what God says about right and wrong. But when faced with a trial, you don't want to do it God's way. You want to do it your own way. It is like asking Jesus for wisdom about your marriage while you are having an affair with a neighbor. It is a double-mindedness.

The picture I get is being on a tilt-a-whirl. It is being tossed back and forth, unstable, and not anchored. Is that all you want for your life? Jesus wants more for you than that. Humble yourself, admit you have been doing it your way, and turn back toward Jesus. Let Him grow you up so you can **faithfully persevere** through any trial. It is knowing where you are going. With Jesus. Not against Him. That is how to move forward.

And perseverance accomplishes something else in your life. When you persevere through any pain, distress, or long-term challenge, you will be mature, complete and lacking nothing. You will even have joy in the process as a reward at the end for holding on without giving way (James 1:4).

But to move forward with joy on a difficult pathway, you will need one more ingredient in the mix. You will need to release your expectations of acceptable outcomes.

Perseverance requires releasing expectations of acceptable outcomes.

Storms of life hit us sometimes without any warning and through no fault of our own. When we go through such difficulties of life, we all have what we would consider acceptable outcomes—deliverance, healing, getting rid of debt, happy relationships. In our prayers, we often tell God how we want Him to answer that request—setting up expectations of what God should do for us. But those expectations can become hindrances and entanglements if we try to hold onto them too tightly.

> Joy requires us to release our expectation of what is an acceptable outcome. (Jenny Heckman, Just Between Us, Spring 2018, p. 44)

When we approach troubles with expectations of what we think are acceptable outcomes from God and then something else happens, our disappointment and anger can explode like geysers shooting out of an underground chamber. It is okay to ask for specific answers to prayer. But we need to hold onto those expected answers with open fingers. **We must release them to Jesus, and let Him decide what to do.** That is releasing expectations.

You learned in the lesson how Paul did that in 2 Corinthians 12. He wanted to be healed and asked for it three times. When Christ gave His answer as "No," Paul released that expectation of healing and replaced it with praise for having Christ's power displayed in his own weakness.

When you release your expectation of acceptable outcomes, you can rejoice at what God has done or is going to do instead of complaining about what God did not do.

Consider how both Martha and Mary responded to Jesus in John 11, "If you had been here, my brother would not have died." That was their only acceptable outcome. But Jesus had a greater purpose. Jesus loved them (John 11:5) and still let them go through that pain. They did nothing wrong. He wept with them. But He had a greater purpose than theirs. When Martha and Mary saw Him, they had to trust His goodness in whatever He would do for them in their trouble. What would be His acceptable outcome? Bringing a four-day dead Lazarus back to life was a far better outcome than what the sisters had in mind.

You can avoid the trap of unreleased expectations. You do that by releasing them. By faith, you can know with certainty that Jesus loves you and knows what is going on in your life. You can have confidence in His power to do something about it. But **the way to release**

expectations is to trust in His goodness in whatever He chooses to do in that situation.

It is okay to ask for your heart's desire. But leave the decision in His hands. Accept the outcome that He provides. In adversity, God can avert the trouble, He can deliver you from it, or He can allow you to suffer through it. Let Him fill your heart with joy in whatever He chooses to do.

What trials are you going through right now? What do you expect to happen as acceptable outcomes? It is time to release those expectations and stay on the right pathway to a joyful walk.

Perseverance is a choice.

We live in a fallen world. Bad things will happen. Life will be challenging and hard at times. If we are going to faithfully persevere, you and I are going to have to accept this—not like it, but recognize it and not be discouraged. God is working during this time in history. He says to us, "Okay I am going to use those very things, those tough things to develop something in you, my daughters, so you can get through life successfully. And I will give you my joy during the process." Do you believe Him?

When James wrote that you will know that the testing of your faith develops perseverance, this "knowing" is gained through living it, not head knowledge gained through reading about it. You can read this and believe that it is true in your mind. But until you have experienced it yourself or walked with a friend through a trial so you can see it is real, it just sounds like pie-in-the-sky, churchy kind of thinking.

Remember how I said that if we let Jesus do it, He will remove that not-so-beautiful stuff and strengthen what is left so we can faithfully persevere and have joy in the process—if we let Him. There is a choice to not let Him.

You have to choose perseverance for it to finish its work. What would be the opposite? Whining, complaining, grumbling, anger at God, and giving up. The opposite would also be using an acceptable but unbiblical practice of your culture to fix it—whatever 'it' is. We forget where we are going with Jesus. We move, change jobs, divorce, avoid, blame, consider ourselves victims, buy our way out, drink and drug our way out. You have probably seen your friends do this. Maybe you have done it. I know I have.

But if we let Him, Jesus will remove that yucky stuff to make us mature and complete, not lacking in anything **needed**. What does that mean? It means having what is necessary to live out Jesus' life in us on our faith walks. It does not mean perfect. We are not promised perfection in this life. But God will finish **His** particular work in us before He takes us home.

For you and me, God has things for us to do, kingdom work to do here on earth, during this time between Genesis 3 and Revelation 21. And He needs us to be mature. To be grown up. It is hard work to grow up.

God allows things in our lives to test us, but His motive is not to trip us up. It is not to make us fail, although our choosing to do so is always a possibility. He allows us to share our needs with Him but wants us to release our expectations of acceptable outcomes and trust His goodness in whatever He chooses to do.

We can know what perseverance looks like when we see the example of our Lord. He endured pain, shame, opposition, and so much more. When we look at His example, we can keep moving forward in our storms of life and not grow weary or lose heart.

Perseverance is a gift.

We can ask Jesus to give us His perseverance (2 Thessalonians 3:5). The Holy Spirit can deliver that to us as a gift from God when we need it. With Christ, you are never left on your own to handle anything.

Be tenacious to hold onto Jesus. Keep walking forward when the storms of life try to knock you down. Go wherever Jesus leads you. Persevere. Focus on what He is doing in the midst of what you are doing. Listen to His voice, drowning out all the others. Even when it hurts. When you are tired. When you want to give up. When you want to settle for less. Believe it or not, persevering through the really tough times will lead to a joyful walk of life with Him.

To have a joyful walk, you need to know Christ and God's marvelous grace to you. You need to grasp who you are as a Christian and choose whom you serve every day. You need to claim your freedom from legalism that tries to keep you in chains. You need to keep the eyes of your heart focused on Jesus so you can move forward with perseverance through every trial that comes your way. The reward is a joyful walk with Christ for a lifetime.

Let Jesus satisfy your heart with joy so that your daily walk with Him will be a joyful one.

Reflect

What expectations of acceptable outcomes have you been holding tightly in your spiritual hands?

Consider releasing them and start rejoicing at what God has done or is going to do instead of complaining about what God did not do.

Pray: *Thank God for whatever you are facing today. Ask Him to help you release your expectations of acceptable outcomes so they do not become a hindrance to having a joyful faith walk with Him. Tell Him you will trust His goodness in whatever He chooses to do in that trouble or suffering.*

The Believer's Identity in Christ

These benefits are yours from the moment you trusted in Jesus Christ for salvation. You are...

1	JUSTIFIED (DECLARED RIGHTEOUS) *"For all have sinned and fall short of the glory of God, and are **justified freely by his grace** through the redemption that came by Christ Jesus." (Romans 3:23-24)*
2	MADE AT PEACE WITH GOD *"Therefore, since we have been justified by faith, **we have peace with God** through our Lord Jesus Christ." (Romans 5:1)*
3	SAFE FROM THE WRATH OF GOD *"Since we have now been justified by his blood, **how much more shall we be saved from God's wrath through him.**" (Romans 5:9)*
4	RECONCILED TO GOD *"For if, when we were God's enemies, **we were reconciled to him through the death of his Son**, how much more, having been reconciled, shall we be saved through his life." (Romans 5:10)*
5	REDEEMED *"In him **we have redemption through his blood**, the forgiveness of sins, in accordance with the riches of God's grace." (Ephesians 1:7)*
6	FREED FROM CONDEMNATION (JUDGMENT) *"Therefore, there is now **no condemnation** for those who are in Christ Jesus." (Romans 8:1) "**Whoever believes in him is not condemned**, but whoever does not believe stands condemned already because he has not believed in the name of God's one and only Son." (John 3:18)*
7	INDWELT BY THE HOLY SPIRIT *"You, however, are controlled not by the sinful nature but by the Spirit, if the Spirit of God lives in you. And if anyone does not have the Spirit of Christ, he does not belong to Christ." (Romans 8:9)*
8	ADOPTED AS SONS *"because those who are led by the Spirit of God are sons of God...**you received the Spirit of sonship. And by him,** we cry out, 'Abba! Father!'" (Romans 8:14-15)*
9	ACCEPTED BY GOD *"Accept one another, then, **just as Christ accepted you**, in order to bring praise to God." (Romans 15:7)*
10	BAPTIZED INTO CHRIST'S BODY (THE CHURCH) *"For **we were all baptized by one Spirit into one body** —whether Jews or Greeks, slave or free — and we were all given the one Spirit to drink." (1 Corinthians 12:13)*
11	CHOSEN BY GOD *"For **he chose us in him** before the creation of the world to be holy and blameless in his sight." (Ephesians 1:4)*

12	SAVED BY GRACE *"For it is **by grace you have been saved,** though faith — and this not from yourselves, it is the gift of God — not by works, so that no one can boast." (Ephesians 2:8-9)*
13	GOD HAS BEEN PROPITIATED (SATISFIED) *"he is the **atoning sacrifice for our sins**, and not only for ours but also for the sins of the whole world." (1 John 2:2)*
14	FREED FROM THE LAW *"So my brothers, **you also were died to the Law** through the body of Christ, that you might belong to another, to him who was raised from the dead, that we might bear fruit to God." (Romans 7:4)*
15	TRANSLATED OUT OF DARKNESS INTO LIGHT *"For you were once darkness, but **now you are light in the Lord**. Live as children of light." (Ephesians 5:8)*
16	FORGIVEN *"When you were dead in your sins and in the uncircumcision of your sinful nature, God made you alive with Christ. He **forgave us all our sins**, having cancelled the written code, with its regulations, that was against us and that stood opposed to us; he took it away, nailing it to the cross." (Colossians 2:13-14)*
17	WASHED CLEAN *"And that is what some of you were. But **you were washed**, you were sanctified, you were justified in the name of the Lord Jesus Christ and by the Spirit of our God." (1 Corinthians 6:11)*
18	MADE HOLY AND BLAMELESS *"But now he has reconciled you by Christ's physical body through death to present you **holy in his sight, without blemish and free from accusation...**" (Colossians 1:22)*
19	SEALED IN CHRIST *"And you also were included in Christ when you heard the word of truth...Having believed, **you were marked in him with a seal, the promised Holy Spirit**, who is a deposit guaranteeing our inheritance until the redemption of those who are God's own possession..." (Ephesians 1:13-14)*
20	CLOTHED WITH CHRIST *"For all of you who were baptized into Christ have **clothed yourselves with Christ**." (Galatians 3:27)*
21	GIVEN CHRIST'S RIGHTEOUSNESS *"God made him who had no sin to be sin for us, so that **in him we might become the righteousness of God**." (2 Corinthians 5:21)*
22	MADE INTO A TEMPLE OF THE HOLY SPIRIT *"Do you not know that **your body is a temple of the Holy Spirit, who is in you, whom you have received from God? You are not your own?**" (1 Corinthians 6:19)*
23	MADE PERFECT FOREVER *"Because by one sacrifice he has **made perfect forever** those who are being made holy." (Hebrews 10:14)*

24	TRANSLATED OUT OF DEATH INTO LIFE *"I tell you the truth, whoever hears my word and believes in him who sent me **has eternal life** and will not be condemned; he **has crossed over from death into life.**" (John 5:24) "As for you, you were **dead** in your transgressions and sins...But because of his great love for us, God, who is rich in mercy, **made us alive with Christ** even when we were **dead** in transgressions..." (Ephesians 2:1,4-5)*
25	BORN AGAIN *"Praise be to the God and Father of our Lord Jesus Christ! In his great mercy, **he has given us new birth** into a living hope through the resurrection of Jesus Christ from the dead." (1 Peter 1:3)*
26	SANCTIFIED (MADE HOLY) *"And by that will, **we have been made holy** through the sacrifice of the body of Jesus Christ once for all." (Hebrews 10:10) "And that is what some of you were. But you were washed, **you were sanctified**, you were justified in the name of the Lord Jesus Christ and by the Spirit of our God." (1 Corinthians 6:11)*
27	MADE A NEW CREATION *"Therefore, if anyone is in Christ, **he is a new creation**; the old has gone, the new has come!" (2 Corinthians 5:17)* *"For we are **God's workmanship, created in Christ Jesus** to do good works, which God prepared in advance for us to do." (Ephesians 2:10)*
28	MADE CHILDREN OF GOD *"Yet to all who received him, to those who believed in his name, he gave the right to become **children of God**..." (John 1:12)*
29	MADE COMPLETE *"For in Christ all the fullness of the Deity lives in bodily form, **you have been given fullness in Christ**..." (Colossians 2:9-10)*
30	MADE HEIRS OF GOD *"Now if we are children, then **we are heirs — heirs of God and co-heirs with Christ**," (Romans 8:17) "...since you are a son, **God has made you also an heir**." (Galatians 4:7)*
31	MADE CITIZENS OF HEAVEN *"But **our citizenship is in heaven**. And we eagerly await a Savior from there, the Lord Jesus Christ, who, by the power that enables him to bring everything under his control, will transform our lowly bodies so that they will be like his glorious body." (Philippians 3:20-21)*
32	MADE INTO A HOLY AND ROYAL PRIESTHOOD *"To him who loves us and has ... made us to be a **kingdom and priests to serve his God and Father**..." (Revelation 1:5b-6) "You also, like living stones, are being built into a spiritual house to be a **holy priesthood, offering spiritual sacrifices** acceptable to God through Jesus Christ . . . But you are a chosen people, a **royal priesthood**, a holy nation, a people belonging to God," (1 Peter 2:5,9)*

33	GIVEN CONFIDENT ACCESS TO GOD *"In him and through faith in him **we may approach God with freedom and confidence.**" (Ephesians 3:12) "Therefore, brothers, since **we have confidence to enter the Most Holy Place** by the blood of Jesus, … **let us draw near to God with a sincere heart in full assurance of faith**,." (Hebrews 10:19-23)*
34	WE HAVE BEEN GIVEN EVERY SPIRITUAL BLESSING *"Praise be the God and Father of our Lord Jesus Christ, who has blessed us in the heavenly realms with **every spiritual blessing** in Christ." (Ephesians 1:3) "his divine power has given us **everything we need for life and godliness** through our knowledge of him who called us by his own glory and goodness." (2 Peter 1:3)*
35	NEVER SEPARATED FROM GOD'S LOVE *"For I am convinced that neither death nor life, neither angels nor demons, neither the present nor the future, nor any powers, neither height nor depth, nor anything else in all creation, **will be able to separate us** from the love of God that is in Christ Jesus our Lord." (Romans 8:38-39)*
36	UNITED WITH CHRIST *"For if we have been **united** with him in a death like his, we will certainly also be **united** with him in a resurrection like his." (Romans 6:5)*

Choose 7 of the benefits in the list above that are most meaningful to you and write them on your ID card below. Take a picture of your ID card to remind you of your identity in Christ.

MY IDENTITY IN CHRIST

_____, *Child of God, Saint*

DOB: _____

1. _____
2. _____
3. _____
4. _____
5. _____
6. _____
7. _____

The Biblical Process for Dealing with Recognized Sin

1. View yourself rightly.

Your identity is not "_____" (coveter, greedy, gossiper, whatever that sin is). You are in Christ, a child of God, who sometimes "_____" (covets, is greedy, gossips, etc.).

2. Agree with God (confess) that you are guilty of that behavior.

To **confess** biblically means *to agree with God about what you and He both know to be true.* Confession is not a formula, a process, or dependent on a mediator. Regarding sin in your life, it is not saying, "I'm sorry." It is saying, "I agree with you, God. I blew it!" You see your sin as something awful! Your sin is already forgiven.

Use grumbling as an example: You read Philippians 2:14, "Do everything without grumbling or arguing." The Spirit convicts you that you grumble and complain a lot. You agree with God that your grumbling is not pleasing to Him—in fact, He hates it. Grumbling doesn't fit someone who is in Christ, representing Christ to the world. That is **confession.**

3. Choose obedience (repentance).

Repentance means *to change your mind about that sin, to mourn its ugliness, resulting in changing your actions.* It is saying, "I recognize what I am doing is wrong. This fills me with sorrow because it displeases you, God. Please help me to live differently." Decide you want to live by the Spirit's power in that area of your life.

For grumbling: You want to live in order to please God, and God wants you to stop grumbling and complaining. It comes from a heart that feels entitled and not grateful. So you pray, "Lord Jesus, please have your Spirit nudge me when I am grumbling and complaining. Help me to say no to the temptation and to give up that habit of being ungrateful. By faith, Lord, I want you to do that in my life." That is **repentance.**

4. Depend on the Spirit's power.

Our Lord Jesus Christ is not interested in our compliance or outward conformity as much as He desires our obedience from the heart. Consider saying, *"Lord Jesus, I cannot do this, but you can do this in my life. I trust your Spirit to do this in me."* Depend on the Holy Spirit inside you for that change to take place, whatever it is. Then, watch what He does!

For grumbling: Memorize Philippians 2:14 and James 5:9 and any other scriptures that deal with not grumbling and being grateful instead. Be sensitive to the Spirit's nudging when you are tempted to do that. Desire a life that pleases God. It's okay to say, "Lord Jesus, I can't do this on my own. I trust you to do this in me and through me." Then, watch what He does! That is **dependence.**

The Holy Spirit's Empowering Presence

We cannot see the Holy Spirit inside of us. But we know he is working inside us because we become aware of the evidence. These are some of the things the Spirit does for us:

> **He helps us understand what the Bible teaches.** Has someone explained something to you about the Bible, and you understood what she was saying? That is the Spirit inside of you helping you to understand. *John 16:13; 1 Cor. 2:13*

> **He gives us the words to tell others about Jesus and say that Jesus is God.** Have you wanted to tell someone about Jesus but did not know what to say, then all of a sudden, the words just popped into your head for you to tell that person about Jesus? That is the Holy Spirit living inside of you prompting you with the right words to say. *John 14:26; 1 Corinthians 12:3*

> **He gives us assurance that we are God's children.** Have you ever felt really loved by God? That is the Spirit inside of you letting you know for sure that you are God's child, and He loves you. *Romans 8:16*

> **He makes us want to do what pleases God.** Do you have a desire to please God with your life? That is the Holy Spirit inside of you giving you that desire. *Romans 12:11; Jer. 31:31,33*

> **He helps us to feel joy as we serve Jesus and when we do the right things.** Have you ever felt really good when you chose to do the right thing or chose to be helpful? That is the Holy Spirit inside of you letting you feel God's pleasure. *Romans 14:17-18*

> **He makes us want to avoid doing what does not please God.** Have you ever felt something tugging at you inside when you were tempted to do something wrong? That is the Holy Spirit living inside of you nudging you, reminding you what does not please God so you can choose not to do that. We can ask him to let us know in our thinking or feelings when we are tempted to do something bad. He promises to do that. *Galatians 5:16*

➢ **He makes us to become more like Jesus, especially in loving other people.** Have you ever started loving someone even more after you started praying for him/her? That is the Holy Spirit living inside of you doing that. *Galatians 5:22-23*

➢ **He makes us want to sing praises to God, in our hearts and out loud, and be thankful for God's goodness.** Do you like to sing praises to God? Do you feel thankful to God for his goodness to you? That is the Spirit living inside of you filling your heart with praise and thanksgiving to God. *Ephesians 5:18-20*

➢ **He prays for us when we need help or do not know how to pray.** Have you ever had a huge problem and did not know what to ask God to do about it, but God took care of the problem anyway? That is the Holy Spirit living inside of you working to take care of your need before you even ask. *Romans 8:26-27*

Which of the above evidences have you recognized in your life?

Prayer: Thank God for specific ways and times His Spirit has worked in your life. Ask Him to make you more aware of His empowering presence in you.

Sources

The following resources were used in the preparation and writing of this study.

1. "Even If" by Mercy Me

2. *Graceful Living Bible Study* by Melanie Newton

3. *Growing in Grace* by Bob George

4. Jenny Heckman, *Just Between Us* magazine, Spring 2018

5. *The NIV Study Bible New International Version,* Zondervan Bible Publishers, 1985.

6. "What a Beautiful Name" by Ben Fielding and Brooke Ligertwood

7. It's a Walk" (accessed on August 20, 2020 at mintools.com/blog/christian-life-walk.htm)